HMH | (into) Math™

Practice and Homework Journal

Grade 1

Currency and Coins Photos courtesy of United States Mint, Bureau of Engraving and Houghton Mifflin Harcourt

Printed in the U.S.A.

ISBN 978-0-358-11099-6

9 10 11 12 0909 28 27 26 25 24 23

4500865337   C D E F G

Ways to Add and Subtract

Module 4 Apply the Addition and Subtraction Relationship

Unit 2 Addition and Subtraction Situations and Data

Module 7 Understand Compare Problems

Module 8 Data

Unit 3 Numbers to 120

Addition and Subtraction in Base Ten

Unit 5 Geometry

Module 14 Three-Dimensional Shapes

Module 15 Two-Dimensional Shapes

Module 16 Fraction Foundations

Unit 6 Measurement

© Houghton Mifflin Harcourt Publishing Company

Represent Addition

(MP) **Model with Mathematics**

Write an equation to solve.

1 Kelly eats 5 green grapes and 4 red grapes.
How many grapes does Kelly eat?

_____ + _____ = _____

_____ grapes

---

2 Kim puts 7 books on the table.
Then she puts 6 more books on the table.
How many books are on the table now?

_____ + _____ = _____

_____ books

---

3 **Open Ended** Jamal and Kim
have a total of 10 plants.
Write an equation to show
how many plants Jamal
and Kim could each have.
Draw to show your thinking.

_____ = _____ + _____

Add. Write the sum.

4 7 + 7 = _____   **5** 9 + 6 = _____   **6** _____ = 1 + 8

Test Prep

Fill in the bubble next to the correct answer.

7 There are 8 ducks on the pond.
Then 5 more ducks fly to the pond.
How many ducks are there now?

○ 3 ducks

○ 12 ducks

○ 13 ducks

8 1 tree is tall. 7 trees are short.
Which equation shows
how many trees there are?

○ $7 = 6 + 1$ ○ $8 = 1 + 7$ ○ $9 = 1 + 8$

9 7 fish swim. 8 fish join them.
Which equation shows
how many fish swim now?

○ $7 + 1 = 8$ ○ $7 + 8 = 15$ ○ $10 + 7 = 17$

Spiral Review

10 Count the number of ants.
Write the number.

_____

Count On

Count on to add.

1 (MP) **Construct Arguments**

Jody counts on to solve 1 + 7.
Explain why Jody should start at 7.

_____

_____

2 (MP) **Model with Mathematics**

Ian has 6 small carrots and 3 big carrots.
Write an equation to show
how many carrots he has.

_____ + _____ = _____

Ian has _____ carrots.

3 **Math on the Spot** Which three numbers
can you use to complete the equation?

Jennifer has ■ stamps.
She gets ■ more stamps.
How many stamps does she have now?

_____ + _____ = _____

Jennifer has _____ stamps now.

4 9 + 1 = _____   **5** 5 + 2 = _____   **6** _____ = 3 + 8

Test Prep

Fill in the bubble next to the correct answer.

7 Count on to solve.
Which is the sum of 9 + 3?

○ 12   ○ 11   ○ 6

8 There are 2 frogs on a lily pad.
Then 7 more frogs join them.
How many frogs are on the lily pad now?
Count on to solve.

○ 8 frogs   ○ 9 frogs   ○ 10 frogs

9 There are 8 birds in a tree.
1 bird is in a bush.
How many birds are there?
Count on to solve.

○ 7 birds   ○ 8 birds   ○ 9 birds

Spiral Review

Write an equation to solve.

10 Lana holds 4 coins in one hand
and 6 coins in her other hand.
How many coins does she hold?

_____ + _____ = _____

_____ coins

Add 10 and More

Draw ⬤ to show your work.

1 (MP) **Use Tools** Ginger has 10 caps.
Then she gets 2 more caps.
How many caps does she have now?

_____ + _____ = _____

Ginger has _____ caps now.

2 Draw ⬤ to show 10. Draw ⬤ to show 4.
Complete the equation to model the picture.

10 + _____ = _____

Add.

3 10 + 7 = _____

4 10 + 3 = _____

5 10 + 9 = _____

6 10 + 8 = _____

7 _____ = 10 + 6

8 _____ = 10 + 0

Test Prep

Fill in the bubble next to the correct answer.

9 Which equation matches the picture?

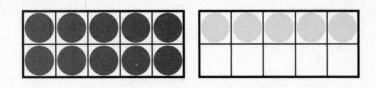

○ 5 + 5 = 10   ○ 10 + 5 = 15   ○ 10 + 10 = 20

10 Which is the sum?

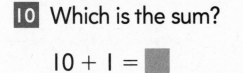

10 + 1 = ▮

○ 9   ○ 11   ○ 20

11 Derrick has 10 candles.
Then he buys 6 more candles.
How many candles does he have now?

○ 4 candles   ○ 11 candles   ○ 16 candles

Spiral Review

Count on to add.

12 Gina has 2 red hats and 7 blue hats.
How many hats does Gina have?

_____ hats

13 9 + 3 = _____   **14** 7 + 1 = _____

Name _____

Make a Ten to Add

1 **Open Ended** Write an equation to match the picture.

_____ + _____ = _____

2 Show how to make a ten to add 8 + 5. Draw ⬤ to show your thinking.

8 + _____ + _____ = ▢

10 + _____ = _____

So, 8 + 5 = _____.

MP **Use Structure** Make a ten to add.

3 What is 7 + 5?

7 + _____ + _____ = ▢

10 + _____ = _____

So, 7 + 5 = _____.

4 What is 9 + 9?

9 + _____ + _____ = ▢

10 + _____ = _____

So, 9 + 9 = _____.

© Houghton Mifflin Harcourt Publishing Company

Test Prep

Fill in the bubble next to the correct answer.

5 Which has the same sum as 8 + 4?

○ 10 + 6   ○ 10 + 3   ○ 10 + 2

6 Which shows how to make a ten
to add 5 + 9?

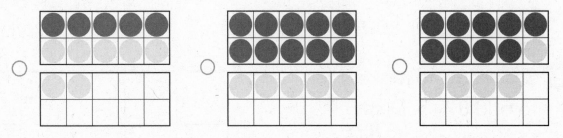

○   ○   ○

Spiral Review

Write an equation to solve the problem.

7 Morgan picks 10 strawberries.
His mother picks 4 strawberries.
How many strawberries do they pick?

_____ + _____ = _____

_____ strawberries

Add.

8 10 + 7 = _____

9 10 + 5 = _____

10 _____ = 10 + 2

11 _____ = 10 + 9

© Houghton Mifflin Harcourt Publishing Company

Name _____

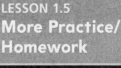
Add Doubles

1 **Use Structure** Tia sees 3 goats.
She also sees 3 cows.
How many animals does she see?
Write the doubles fact. Solve.

Goats   Cows

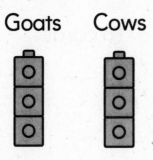

_____ + _____ = _____

Tia sees _____ animals.

2 **Open Ended** Two teams play soccer.
Each team has the same number of girls.
How many girls could be on the teams in all?
Write a doubles fact to show your thinking.

_____ + _____ = _____

_____ girls

Add.

3 $1 + 1 =$ _____

4 $9 + 9 =$ _____

5 $4 + 4 =$ _____

6 _____ $= 2 + 2$

7 _____ $= 6 + 6$

8 _____ $= 7 + 7$

Test Prep

Fill in the bubble next to the correct answer.

9 Kaden makes 8 greeting cards on Tuesday. He makes the same number of cards on Wednesday. How many cards does he make?

　○ 4 cards 　　　○ 14 cards 　　　○ 16 cards

10 Which is the sum of the doubles fact?

$5 + 5 = $ ▊

　○ 8 　　　　　○ 10 　　　　　○ 12

Spiral Review

Make a ten to solve.
Draw ● **to show your thinking.**

11 Tommy eats 9 grapes.
Then he eats another 3 grapes.
How many grapes does he eat?

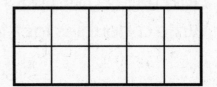

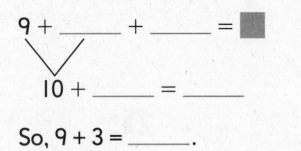

$9 +$ _____ $+$ _____ $=$ ▊

$10 +$ _____ $=$ _____

So, $9 + 3 =$ _____ .

Tommy eats _____ grapes.

LESSON 1.6
**More Practice/
Homework**

 **ONLINE**
Video Tutorials and
Interactive Examples

Use Known Sums to Add

1 Use a doubles fact to add 4 + 5.

$4 + 4 =$ _____

So, $4 + 5 =$ _____ .

2 Use a doubles fact to add 6 + 5.

$5 + 5 =$ _____

So, $6 + 5 =$ _____ .

3 **Math on the Spot** Brianna has 8 toy ducks.
Ian has the same number of toy ducks
and a toy fish. How many toys do
Brianna and Ian have?

_____ toys

4 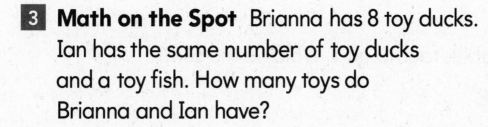 **Construct Arguments** Ted has 7 shells.
Then he finds 8 more shells.
How many shells does he have now?
Explain how to use a doubles fact to solve.

Ted has _____ shells now.

_____

_____

Test Prep

Fill in the bubble next to the correct answer.

5 Tyler has 6 toy dogs.
Maya has 7 toy dogs.
How many toy dogs do they have?

  ○ 11 toy dogs   ○ 13 toy dogs   ○ 15 toy dogs

6 Use a doubles fact to add. Which is the sum?

$3 + 4 = \blacksquare$

  ○ 7   ○ 8   ○ 9

7 Use a doubles fact to add. Which is the sum?

$8 + 7 = \blacksquare$

  ○ 13   ○ 15   ○ 17

Spiral Review

Write the doubles fact. Solve.

8 James counts 4 people in the deli.
Then 4 more people walk in.
How many people are in the deli now?

_____ + _____ = _____   _____ people

Add.

9 $6 + 6 =$ _____   **10** $5 + 5 =$ _____   **11** _____ $= 9 + 9$

LESSON 1.7
**More Practice/
Homework**

 **ONLINE**
Video Tutorials and
Interactive Examples

Choose a Strategy to Add

1 (MP) **Construct Arguments**
Choose a strategy you can use
to add $9 + 8$. Draw or write
to show how the strategy works.

2 **Open Ended** Write two numbers
to complete the word problem.
Then use any strategy to solve.

_____ birds are in a tree.

_____ more birds fly there.

How many birds are in the tree now?

_____ birds

Use any strategy to add.

3 $4 + 7 = $ _____ **4** $6 + 3 = $ _____ **5** $9 + 5 = $ _____

Test Prep

Fill in the bubble next to the correct answer.

6 Juan has 8 blocks.
Tina has the same number of blocks.
How many blocks do they have?
Use any strategy to solve.

○ 4 blocks

○ 14 blocks

○ 16 blocks

7 There are 6 red flowers
and 7 yellow flowers in a vase.
How many flowers are in the vase?
Use any strategy to solve.

○ 15 flowers   ○ 13 flowers   ○ 11 flowers

Spiral Review

8 Jenny eats 7 grapes. Then she eats 2 more.
How many grapes does she eat?
Draw jumps on the number line to count on.

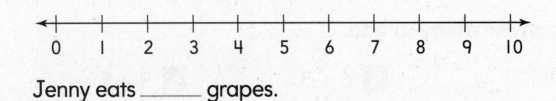

Jenny eats _____ grapes.

Name _____

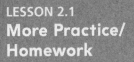
Represent Subtraction

Write an equation to solve.

1  **Model with Mathematics**
There are 4 bears in the woods.
Then 1 bear walks away.
How many bears are there now?

_____ − _____ = _____

_____ bears

2 Open Ended Ray has 11 peaches.
Then he gives some away.
How many peaches could he have now?
Draw to show your thinking.

11 − _____ = _____

_____ peaches

Subtract. Write the difference.

3 6 − 3 = _____

4 9 − 2 = _____

5 _____ = 10 − 7

6 _____ = 12 − 6

Test Prep

Fill in the bubble next to the correct answer.

7 9 fish are under the boat.
Then 5 fish swim away.

Which equation shows how many
fish are under the boat now?

- ○ $9 - 5 = 4$
- ○ $5 - 4 = 1$
- ○ $9 + 5 = 14$

8 There are 13 books on a table.
5 books fall on the ground.
How many books are on the table now?

- ○ 18 books
- ○ 8 books
- ○ 6 books

Spiral Review

Add.

9 $3 + 3 = $ _____

10 $8 + 8 = $ _____

11 $4 + 4 = $ _____

12 $7 + 7 = $ _____

Name _____

Count Back

1 (MP) **Use Tools** Sasha has 8 erasers.
She gives 3 erasers to Ben.
How many erasers does Sasha have now?
Draw jumps to show your thinking.

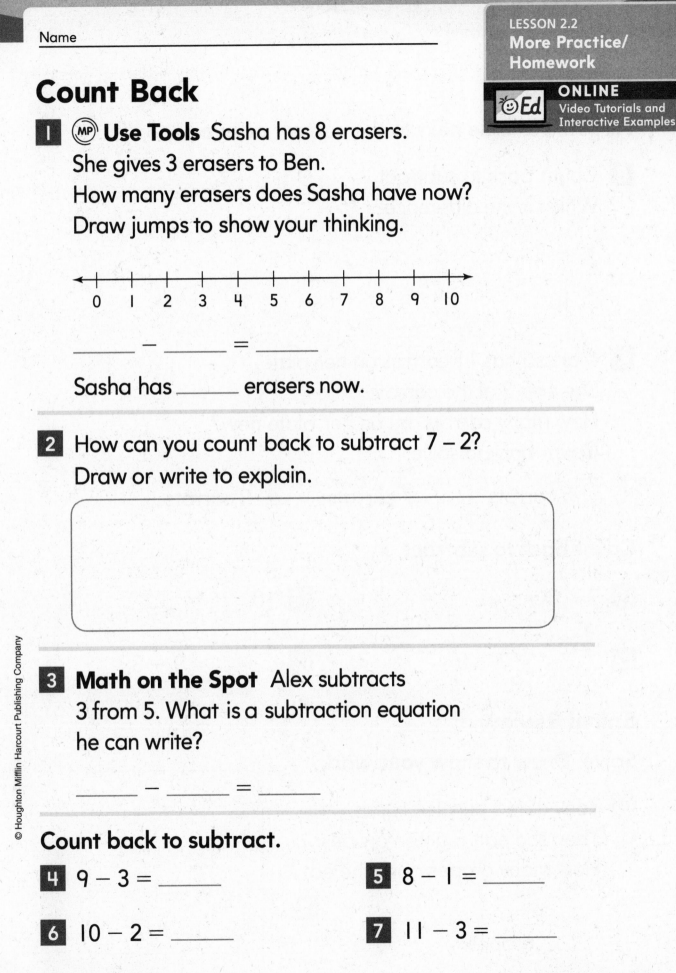

```
<----+----+----+----+----+----+----+----+----+----+---->
     0    1    2    3    4    5    6    7    8    9    10
```

_____ – _____ = _____

Sasha has _____ erasers now.

2 How can you count back to subtract 7 – 2?
Draw or write to explain.

3 **Math on the Spot** Alex subtracts
3 from 5. What is a subtraction equation
he can write?

_____ – _____ = _____

Count back to subtract.

4 9 – 3 = _____

5 8 – 1 = _____

6 10 – 2 = _____

7 11 – 3 = _____

Test Prep

Fill in the bubble next to the correct answer.

8 Count back to subtract.
Which is the difference?

$12 - 3 =$ ▢

○ 10   ○ 9   ○ 7

---

9 Marissa has 11 carrots on her plate.
She eats 2 of the carrots.
How many carrots are on her plate now?
Count back to solve.

○ 5 carrots   ○ 7 carrots   ○ 9 carrots

Count back to subtract.

10 $7 - 3 =$ _____

11 $10 - 1 =$ _____

12 _____ $= 7 - 0$

13 _____ $= 9 - 3$

Spiral Review

Solve. Draw to show your work.

14 Zoey eats 5 purple grapes.
Then she eats 6 green grapes.
How many grapes does she eat?

_____ grapes

Name _____

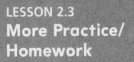
Count On to Subtract

Count on to subtract.

1 **Model with Mathematics**
Olga has 6 ladybug stamps.
5 of them are in her bag.
The rest are on her desk.
How many ladybug stamps
are on her desk?

_____ – _____ = _____

_____ ladybug stamp

2 (MP) **Construct Arguments** Nick wants to
subtract 11 – 8. Explain how he can count on
to find the difference.

_____

_____

_____

_____

Count on to subtract.

3 12 – 9 = _____   **4** 10 – 8 = _____

5 8 – 7 = _____   **6** 9 – 7 = _____

Test Prep

Fill in the bubble next to the correct answer.

7 Jan has 10 tickets. 7 are for a play.
The rest of them are for a movie.
Count on to subtract.
How many tickets are for a movie?

○ 3 tickets   ○ 4 tickets   ○ 17 tickets

8 Grady has 7 apples.
6 are red. The rest are green.
Count on to subtract.
How many apples are green?

○ 13 apples   ○ 2 apples   ○ 1 apple

9 Count on to subtract.
Which is $8 - 6$?

○ 1   ○ 2   ○ 3

Spiral Review

Count back to subtract.

10 $11 - 3 =$ _____

11 $6 - 1 =$ _____

12 _____ $= 8 - 2$

13 _____ $= 10 - 0$

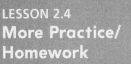

Add to Subtract

Add to subtract.

1 13 goats are at the farm.
9 of them eat. The rest play.
How many goats play?

13 − 9 = [ ]

9 + _____ = 13

So, 13 − 9 = _____ .

_____ goats play.

---

2 What is 10 − 8?

8 + _____ = 10

So, 10 − 8 = _____ .

Write addition and subtraction equations to solve.

3 (MP) **Model with Mathematics**
Jo has 12 boxes. 6 are closed.
The rest of them are open.
How many boxes are open?

_____ + _____ = _____

So, _____ − _____ = _____ .

_____ boxes are open.

Test Prep

Fill in the bubble next to the correct answer.

4 Hayden has 11 pencils.
9 of them are in his bag.
The rest are in his desk.
Which addition fact can be used to find
how many pencils are in his desk?

$11 - 9 = \boxed{}$

○ $1 + 9 = 10$

○ $9 + 2 = 11$

○ $2 + 7 = 9$

5 Justine has 9 ears of corn.
5 are blue. The rest are yellow.
Which addition fact can be used to find
how many ears of corn are yellow?

$9 - 5 = \boxed{}$

○ $5 + 4 = 9$ ○ $4 + 9 = 13$ ○ $9 + 5 = 14$

Spiral Review

Count on to subtract.

6 $10 - 8 =$ _____   **7** $11 - 8 =$ _____

8 $9 - 6 =$ _____   **9** $6 - 5 =$ _____

Name _____

Use 10 to Subtract

1 (MP) **Use Tools** Tanya has 18 roses.
9 of them are red. The rest are white.
How many roses are white?

Use the ten frames to solve.
Draw to show your thinking.

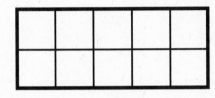 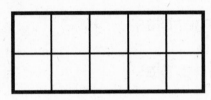

_____ white roses

---

2 (MP) **Construct Arguments** How can you
make a ten to subtract 16 − 8?

_____

_____

_____

Make a ten to subtract.
Draw ● **to show your thinking.**

3 $14 - 5 =$ ▢

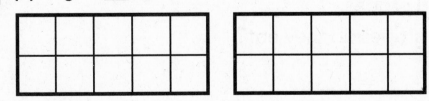

$14 - 5 =$ _____

© Houghton Mifflin Harcourt Publishing Company

Test Prep

Fill in the bubble next to the correct answer.

4 Gary has 13 marbles.
9 are blue. The rest are yellow.
How many yellow marbles does he have?
Make a ten to solve.

○ 4 yellow marbles

○ 5 yellow marbles

○ 6 yellow marbles

5 Which equation matches the picture?

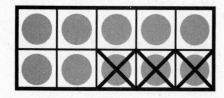 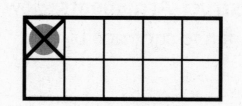

○ 11 − 10 = 1   ○ 7 − 4 = 3   ○ 11 − 4 = 7

Spiral Review

Write an equation to solve.

6 Alexa eats 3 grapes.
Janet eats 4 grapes.
How many grapes do they eat?

_____ + _____ = _____

They eat _____ grapes.

LESSON 2.6
**More Practice/
Homework**

ONLINE
Video Tutorials and
Interactive Examples

Choose a Strategy to Subtract

(MP) Model with Mathematics

Use any strategy to solve.
Write the equation.

1 Cade has 14 buttons.
   5 of them are red.
   The rest are black.
   How many buttons are black?

   _____ – _____ = _____

   _____ buttons are black.

2 Jessica makes 12 cards.
   She mails 5 of them to her family.
   How many cards does she have now?

   _____ – _____ = _____

   Jessica has _____ cards now.

3 Margo has 16 flowers.
   She gives 9 of them to her friend.
   How many does Margo have now?

   _____ – _____ = _____

   Margo has _____ flowers now.

Test Prep

Fill in the bubble next to the correct answer.
Use any strategy to solve.

4 Mike picks 11 pumpkins.
3 are small. The rest are large.
How many pumpkins are large?

○ 7 pumpkins   ○ 8 pumpkins   ○ 14 pumpkins

5 12 girls sit. Then 9 of them stand.
How many girls sit now?

○ 3 girls   ○ 4 girls   ○ 7 girls

Use any strategy to subtract.

6 15 − 9 = _____   **7** 11 − 6 = _____

Spiral Review

Count on to subtract.

8 9 − 7 = _____   **9** 8 − 5 = _____

Add to subtract.

10 What is 10 − 5?

5 + _____ = 10

So, 10 − 5 = _____.

11 What is 8 − 7?

7 + _____ = 8

So, 8 − 7 = _____.

LESSON 3.1
**More Practice/
Homework**

ONLINE
Video Tutorials and
Interactive Examples

Represent Addition in Any Order

Write two addition equations that can be used to solve the problem. Draw pictures to match the equations.

1 (MP) **Reason** There are 2 squirrels in the tree. There are 3 squirrels on the ground. How many squirrels are there?

_____ = _____ + _____

_____ = _____ + _____

_____ squirrels

2 **Math on the Spot** Choose addends to complete the addition equation. Change the order. Write the numbers.

_____ + _____ = 10   _____ + _____ = _____

Write the sum. Change the order of the addends and add again.

3 8 + 7 = _____   _____ + _____ = _____

4 _____ = 9 + 5   _____ = _____ + _____

Test Prep

Fill in the bubble next to the correct answer.

5 Hannah has 7 books. Jake gives her 6 more books. Which equation can you use to find the number of books Hannah has now?

○ $3 + 3 = 6$

○ $6 + 1 = 7$

○ $6 + 7 = 13$

6 Paul sees 4 dogs and 3 cats. To find the number of dogs and cats, he uses $4 + 3 = 7$. Which other addition equation can he use?

○ $3 + 4 = 7$ ○ $3 + 1 = 4$ ○ $4 + 2 = 6$

Spiral Review

Make a ten to solve.

7 Hank has 8 marbles. Ken gives him 3 more marbles. How many marbles does Hank have in all?

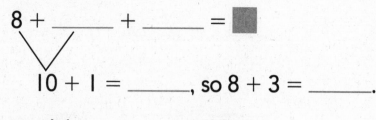

$8 + \underline{\hspace{1cm}} + \underline{\hspace{1cm}} = \blacksquare$

$10 + 1 = \underline{\hspace{1cm}}$, so $8 + 3 = \underline{\hspace{1cm}}$.

Hank has $\underline{\hspace{1cm}}$ marbles.

LESSON 3.2
**More Practice/
Homework**

ONLINE
Video Tutorials and
Interactive Examples

Add in Any Order

Write two addition equations that can be
used to solve the problem.

1 (MP) **Use Repeated Reasoning** Vernon
has 3 big erasers and 6 small erasers.
How many erasers does he have?

_____ = _____ + _____

_____ = _____ + _____

_____ erasers

2 **Math on the Spot** Anna has two groups of
pennies. She has 16 pennies in all. When she
changes the order of the addends, the equation
stays the same. What equation can Anna write?

_____ = _____ + _____

Write the sum. Change the order of the
addends. Add again.

3 $6 + 8 =$ _____

_____ + _____ = _____

4 _____ $= 5 + 4$

_____ $=$ _____ $+$ _____

Test Prep

Fill in the bubble next to the correct answer.

5 Kevin has 5 pencils. Kelly has 3 pencils.
Which equation can you use to find the
number of pencils they have?

○ $5 + 2 = 7$

○ $3 + 5 = 8$

○ $3 + 2 = 5$

6 Mike eats 9 grapes. Then he eats 7 more.
How many grapes does he eat in all?
To find the total number of grapes, Mike
uses $9 + 7 = 16$. Which other addition
equation can he use?

○ $7 + 2 = 9$ ○ $9 + 4 = 13$ ○ $7 + 9 = 16$

Spiral Review

Count on to add.

7 Nicole picks 7 peaches from a tree. Then she
picks 2 more peaches. How many peaches
does she pick?

_____ + _____ = _____

Name _____

LESSON 3.3
**More Practice/
Homework**

Ed **ONLINE**
Video Tutorials and
Interactive Examples

Represent Addition of 3 Numbers

Solve. Draw to show your thinking.

1 (MP) **Reason** Jared feeds 4 goats, 3 lambs, and 6 chickens. How many animals does he feed?

_____ + _____ + _____ = _____

_____ animals

2 **Math on the Spot** I used 📷 📷 📷 to model 3 addends. Use my model. Write the three addends.

My Model

_____ + _____ + _____ = _____

Solve two ways. Circle to group the two addends you will add first.

3 3 + 1 + 4 = ☐

_____ + _____ = _____

So, 3 + 1 + 4 = _____

_____ + _____ = _____

So, 3 + 1 + 4 = _____

Test Prep

Fill in the bubble next to the correct answer.

4 There are 4 large dogs, 3 medium dogs, and 5 small dogs at the park. How many dogs are at the park?

○ 12 dogs

○ 8 dogs

○ 7 dogs

5 Pete adds 5 + 2 + 2. Which shows one way he can use to solve the problem?

○ 5 + 7 = 12   ○ 7 + 2 = 9   ○ 4 + 4 = 8

Spiral Review

Use an addition fact to subtract.

6 Kia has 9 stickers. She gives 4 stickers to her sister. How many stickers does Kia have now?

_____ + _____ = _____

9 − 4 = _____

_____ stickers

© Houghton Mifflin Harcourt Publishing Company

Name _____

Add 3 Numbers

Solve.

1 MP **Use Repeated Reasoning** There are 3 red birds in a tree. There are 5 black birds in the same tree. There is 1 blue bird in the tree. How many birds are in the tree?

_____ birds

Explain how you chose which two addends to add first.

_____

_____

_____

Solve two ways. Circle the addends you add first.

2 $7 + 1 + 3 = $ ▨

_____ + _____ = _____

3 $2 + 4 + 4 = $ ▨

_____ + _____ = _____

$7 + 1 + 3 = $ ▨

_____ + _____ = _____

$2 + 4 + 4 = $ ▨

_____ + _____ = _____

Test Prep

Fill in the bubble next to the correct answer.

4 Linda draws 6 circles, 1 rectangle, and 4 triangles. How many shapes does she draw?

○ 7 shapes   ○ 10 shapes   ○ 11 shapes

5 Bryson adds these 3 numbers. Which shows one way he can use to solve the problem?

$6 + 3 + 3 = \blacksquare$

○ $3 + 3 = 6$

○ $6 + 6 = 12$

○ $9 + 6 = 15$

Spiral Review

Solve.

6 Mr. Jones makes 10 sandwiches. Mrs. Harris makes 9 sandwiches. How many sandwiches do they make?

_____ + _____ = _____

7 $10 + 2 =$ _____

8 $10 + 0 =$ _____

© Houghton Mifflin Harcourt Publishing Company

Name _____

Add 3 Numbers to Solve Problems

Solve. Draw or write to show your thinking.

1 (MP) **Reason** There are 4 children running. There are 3 children skipping. There are 2 children walking. How many children are there?

_____ children

(MP) **Reason** Solve.

2 David sees 2 seals. Then he sees 8 sea lions. Later he sees 4 more seals. How many seals and sea lions does he see?

_____ seals and sea lions

3 Caroline has 3 books. Bob has 1 book. Pete has 4 books. How many books do they have?

_____ books

4 **Math on the Spot** There are 18 pencils. Haley has 6 pencils. Mac has 3 pencils. How many pencils does Sid have?

_____ pencils

Test Prep

Fill in the bubble next to the correct answer.

5 There are 4 big rocks, 3 medium rocks, and 5 small rocks in the yard. How many rocks are there?

○ 12 rocks   ○ 9 rocks   ○ 7 rocks

6 There are 2 butterflies on a plant.
3 more butterflies land on the plant.
Then 6 more butterflies land on the plant.
How many butterflies are on the plant?

○ 9 butterflies   ○ 11 butterflies   ○ 12 butterflies

Spiral Review

Count on to add.

7 There are 6 orange trees. Then 2 more orange trees are planted. How many orange trees are there now?

_____ orange trees

8 Jared has 5 baseball cards. Then he gets 1 more baseball card. How many baseball cards does he have now?

_____ baseball cards

Name _____

LESSON 3.6
More Practice/ Homework

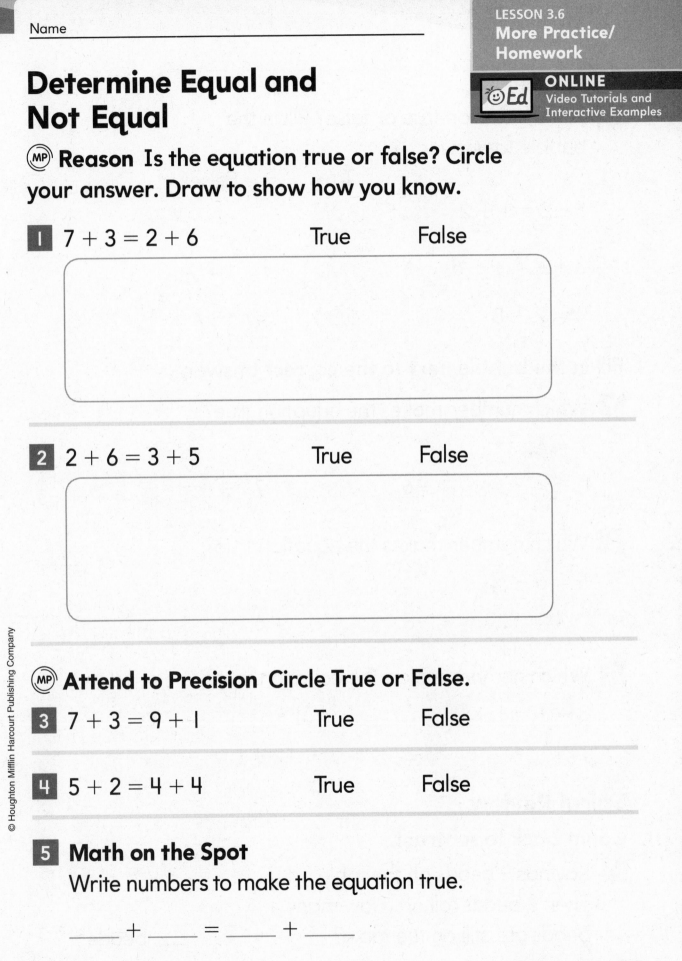

ONLINE
Video Tutorials and
Interactive Examples

Determine Equal and Not Equal

(MP) Reason Is the equation true or false? Circle your answer. Draw to show how you know.

1 $7 + 3 = 2 + 6$ True   False

2 $2 + 6 = 3 + 5$ True   False

(MP) Attend to Precision Circle True or False.

3 $7 + 3 = 9 + 1$ True   False

4 $5 + 2 = 4 + 4$ True   False

5 **Math on the Spot**
Write numbers to make the equation true.

_____ + _____ = _____ + _____

Test Prep

6 Is the equation true or false? Fill in the bubble to answer.

	True	False
$5 - 2 = 1 + 2$	○	○
$3 + 4 = 1 + 6$	○	○
$9 = 2 + 8$	○	○

Fill in the bubble next to the correct answer.

7 Which number makes the equation true?

$7 = \blacksquare$

  ○ 5   ○ 6   ○ 7

8 Which number makes the equation true?

$5 = 6 - \blacksquare$

  ○ 1   ○ 3   ○ 6

9 Which number makes the equation true?

$3 + 1 = 1 + \blacksquare$

  ○ 1   ○ 3   ○ 4

Spiral Review

Count back to subtract.

10 Kay has 9 beads on the table. Then 2 beads roll off. How many beads are still on the table?

_____ beads

Name _____

LESSON 3.7
**More Practice/
Homework**

ONLINE
Video Tutorials and
Interactive Examples

Develop Fluency in Addition

Solve. Write to show two ways to add.

1 (MP) **Use Structure** There are 2 fish with
blue stripes and 6 fish with yellow stripes.
How many fish are there?

____ ◯ ____ = ____   ◯ ☐

_____ fish

---

2 **Math on the Spot** Sam showed how he
added 4 + 2. He made a mistake. Tell how
Sam could find the correct sum.

$$\begin{array}{r} 4 \\ +\ 2 \\ \hline 7 \end{array}$$

_____

_____

Add.

3 $2 + 5 =$ ____   **4** $8 + 2 =$ ____   **5** $6 + 0 =$ ____

---

6 $\begin{array}{r} 7 \\ +\ 1 \\ \hline \end{array}$ **7** $\begin{array}{r} 5 \\ +\ 5 \\ \hline \end{array}$ **8** $\begin{array}{r} 6 \\ +\ 1 \\ \hline \end{array}$ **9** $\begin{array}{r} 0 \\ +\ 0 \\ \hline \end{array}$

Test Prep

Fill in the bubble next to the addition that can be used to solve the problem.

10 There are 6 cats in the barn. 3 more cats come. How many cats are in the barn now?

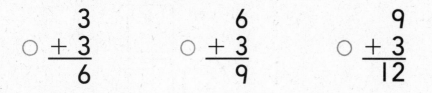

$$\circ \quad \begin{array}{r} 3 \\ +\ 3 \\ \hline 6 \end{array} \qquad \circ \quad \begin{array}{r} 6 \\ +\ 3 \\ \hline 9 \end{array} \qquad \circ \quad \begin{array}{r} 9 \\ +\ 3 \\ \hline 12 \end{array}$$

Spiral Review

Write an equation to solve.

11 There are 7 cats. 5 cats are brown. The rest of the cats are gray. How many cats are gray?

_____ cats are gray.

12 Logan has 4 stickers. Then he gets 3 more stickers. How many stickers does Logan have now?

_____ stickers

Name _____

LESSON 4.1
More Practice/ Homework

🙂Ed **ONLINE**
Video Tutorials and
Interactive Examples

Think Addition to Subtract

(MP) **Model with Mathematics**

Write an addition equation to help you subtract.

1 Gerard has 15 markers. 9 markers have caps. The rest do not have caps. How many markers do not have caps?

_____ + _____ = _____

$15 - 9 =$ _____ _____ markers

2 **Math on the Spot** Carol can use an addition equation to solve a subtraction equation. Write a subtraction equation she can solve using $8 + 9 = 17$.

_____ ◯ _____ ◯ _____

Write an addition equation to help you subtract.

3 What is $12 - 6$?

_____ + _____ = _____

So, $12 - 6 =$ _____ .

4 What is $16 - 7$?

_____ + _____ = _____

So, $16 - 7 =$ _____ .

5 What is $11 - 8$?

_____ + _____ = _____

So, $11 - 8 =$ _____ .

6 What is $14 - 5$?

_____ + _____ = _____

So, $14 - 5 =$ _____ .

Test Prep

Fill in the bubble next to the correct answer.

7 There are 10 kittens in a barn.
7 of them are orange. The rest are gray.

Which addition equation can be used
to help find the number of gray kittens?

$$10 - 7 = \blacksquare$$

○ $10 + 7 = 17$ ○ $3 + 4 = 7$ ○ $7 + 3 = 10$

8 Which addition equation can be used
to help solve $13 - 9 = \blacksquare$?

○ $9 + 4 = 13$ ○ $3 + 9 = 12$ ○ $4 + 5 = 9$

Spiral Review

Count back to subtract.

9 $8 - 3 =$ _____   **10** $7 - 1 =$ _____

11 $11 - 2 =$ _____   **12** $9 - 3 =$ _____

Solve two ways.

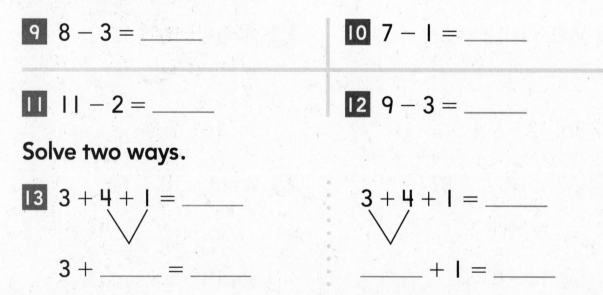

13 $3 + 4 + 1 =$ _____ $3 + 4 + 1 =$ _____

$3 +$ _____ $=$ _____   _____ $+ 1 =$ _____

Name _____

Represent Related Facts

1 (MP) **Model with Mathematics**

There are 15 fish.

8 fish have stripes.

The rest do not have stripes.

How many fish do not have stripes?

_____ fish do not have stripes.

- Write related facts to model the problem.

_____ + _____ = _____   _____ − _____ = _____

_____ + _____ = _____   _____ − _____ = _____

---

2 **Math on the Spot** Circle the equation
that has a mistake. Correct it to
complete the related facts.

$9 + 6 = 15$ $15 + 6 = 9$

$6 + 9 = 15$ $15 - 9 = 6$

_____ ◯ _____ ◯ _____

Complete the related facts.

3 $5 + 6 =$ _____ $11 - 5 =$ _____

$6 +$ _____ $= 11$ _____ − _____ = _____

Test Prep

Fill in the bubble next to the correct answer.

4 Which fact completes the related facts?

$8 + 6 = 14$	$14 - 6 = 8$
	$14 - 8 = 6$

○ $7 + 7 = 14$

○ $2 + 6 = 8$

○ $6 + 8 = 14$

5 Which fact completes the related facts?

$7 + 5 = 12$	$12 - 5 = 7$
$5 + 7 = 12$	

○ $7 - 5 = 2$

○ $12 - 7 = 5$

○ $7 + 2 = 9$

Spiral Review

Make a ten to add.

6 $8 + 4 = $ _____

7 $6 + 9 = $ _____

Circle True or False.

8 $5 + 4 = 10 - 1$ True   False

Name _____

LESSON 4.3
**More Practice/
Homework**

ONLINE
Video Tutorials and
Interactive Examples
Ed

Identify Related Facts

1 **MP** **Reason** Tracy sees 10 kittens.
8 of them play. The other 2 sleep.
Circle two related facts about the kittens.

$$10 + 2 = 12 \qquad 10 - 2 = 8 \qquad 2 + 8 = 10$$

2 **Math on the Spot** Three of these
numbers can be used to write related facts.
Which number cannot be used to write
the related facts? Explain.

13   5   8   7

_____

_____

_____

_____

Solve. Then circle the pairs that are related facts.

3 $6 + 9 =$ _____

$15 - 6 =$ _____

4 $8 + 6 =$ _____

$8 - 6 =$ _____

5 $6 + 7 =$ _____

$7 - 6 =$ _____

6 $7 + 7 =$ _____

$14 - 7 =$ _____

Test Prep

Fill in the bubble next to the correct answer.

7 Colin has 9 rocks.
7 of them are brown.
The rest are black.

Which shows a pair of related facts about the rocks?

○ $9 + 7 = 16$ and $16 - 7 = 9$

○ $7 + 2 = 9$ and $9 - 7 = 2$

○ $9 + 2 = 11$ and $11 - 2 = 9$

8 Which shows a pair of related facts?

○ $4 + 9 = 13$ and $13 - 9 = 4$

○ $9 + 4 = 13$ and $9 - 4 = 5$

○ $5 + 5 = 10$ and $10 + 5 = 15$

Spiral Review

Add.

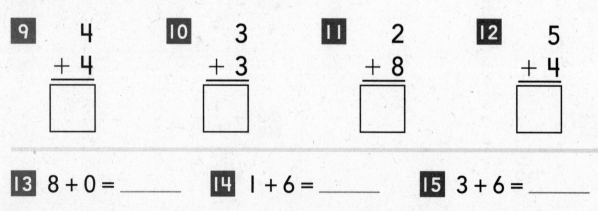

9   4
     $+ 4$

10   3
      $+ 3$

11   2
      $+ 8$

12   5
      $+ 4$

13 $8 + 0 = $ _____   **14** $1 + 6 = $ _____   **15** $3 + 6 = $ _____

Name _____

LESSON 4.4
**More Practice/
Homework**

ONLINE
Video Tutorials and
Interactive Examples

Use Addition to Check Subtraction

Subtract. Then add to check your answer.

1 (MP) **Use Structure** There are 15 children.
8 of them draw. The rest play games.
How many children play games?

15   –   8   = _____

_____ + _____ = _____

_____ children play games.

2 There are 12 lizards in a garden.
4 are brown. The rest are green.
How many green lizards are in the garden?

12   –   4   = _____

_____ + _____ = _____   _____ green lizards

3 There are 11 books on a table. 6 are open.
How many books are closed?

11   –   6   = _____

_____ + _____ = _____

_____ books are closed.

4   12   –   9   = _____

_____ + _____ = _____

5   14   –   8   = _____

_____ + _____ = _____

Test Prep

Fill in the bubble next to the correct answer.

6 Which addition equation can be used
to check the answer to $16 - 8 = \blacksquare$?

○ $4 + 4 = 8$

○ $8 + 8 = 16$

○ $10 + 6 = 16$

7 Marcia solves the equation $16 - 7 = \blacksquare$.
Which addition equation can she use
to check her answer?

○ $2 + 7 = 9$

○ $8 + 8 = 16$

○ $7 + 9 = 16$

Spiral Review

Add.

8 $10 + 3 = $ _____

9 $6 + 6 = $ _____

10 $10 + 6 = $ _____

11 $2 + 8 + 4 = $ _____

LESSON 4.5
**More Practice/
Homework**

ONLINE
Video Tutorials and
Interactive Examples

Use Subtraction to Find an Unknown Addend

Use subtraction to find the unknown addend.

1 (MP) **Use Structure**
5 windows are open.
The rest of them are closed.
There are 12 windows in all.
How many windows are closed?

$5 + \boxed{} = 12$

_____ − _____ = _____

$5 \quad + \text{_____} = \quad 12$

_____ windows are closed.

---

2 Solve $6 + \boxed{} = 11$.

_____ − _____ = _____

$6 \quad + \text{_____} = 11$

3 Solve $9 + \boxed{} = 17$.

_____ − _____ = _____

$9 \quad + \text{_____} = 17$

---

4 Solve $6 + \boxed{} = 13$.

_____ − _____ = _____

$6 \quad + \text{_____} = 13$

5 Solve $9 + \boxed{} = 13$.

_____ − _____ = _____

$9 \quad + \text{_____} = 13$

Test Prep

Fill in the bubble next to the correct answer.

6 Bridget has 6 green blocks and some brown blocks. She has 11 blocks in all.

$6 + \boxed{} = 11$

Which subtraction equation can be used to find the number of brown blocks?

○ $11 - 6 = 5$

○ $11 - 8 = 3$

○ $6 - 5 = 1$

7 Which subtraction equation can be used to solve $8 + \boxed{} = 14$?

○ $8 - 6 = 2$

○ $6 - 2 = 4$

○ $14 - 8 = 6$

Spiral Review

Write the sum.
Change the order of the addends.
Add again.

8 $9 + 3 =$ _____   _____ + _____ = _____

Solve for the Unknown Addend

(MP) **Model with Mathematics**

Write a related subtraction fact to solve.

1 5 chickens eat. The rest sleep.
There are 12 chickens in all.
How many chickens sleep?

$5 +$ ⬛ $= 12$

_____ − _____ = _____

5 + _____ = 12   _____ chickens

2 Rosa has 3 green apples and some
red apples. She has 11 apples in all.
How many red apples does she have?

$3 +$ ⬛ $= 11$

_____ − _____ = _____

3 + _____ = 11   _____ red apples

3 Jen has 7 coins. Max also has some.
They have 15 coins altogether.
How many coins does Max have?

$7 +$ ⬛ $= 15$

_____ − _____ = _____

7 + _____ = 15   _____ coins

Test Prep

Fill in the bubble next to the correct answer.

4 5 panda bears play. The rest nap.
There are 13 panda bears in all.

$5 + \boxed{} = 13$

Which subtraction equation can be used
to find how many panda bears nap?

○ $13 - 5 = 8$

○ $13 - 7 = 6$

○ $8 - 5 = 3$

5 Julie has 9 pinecones. Gabe also has some.
Together they have 17 pinecones.

$9 + \boxed{} = 17$

Which subtraction equation can be used
to find how many pinecones Gabe has?

○ $9 - 8 = 1$ 　　○ $15 - 7 = 8$ 　　○ $17 - 9 = 8$

Spiral Review

Circle true or false.

6 $8 + 2 = 5 + 5$ 　　　　True 　　False

7 $2 + 6 = 6 - 2$ 　　　　True 　　False

© Houghton Mifflin Harcourt Publishing Company

LESSON 4.7
**More Practice/
Homework**

 ONLINE
Video Tutorials and
Interactive Examples

Develop Fluency in Subtraction

Ⓜ️ Model with Mathematics

Write a subtraction equation to solve.

1 10 dogs are at the park.
4 of them leave. How many
dogs are at the park now?

_____ – _____ = _____

_____ dogs

2 Maria has 8 blocks. 4 are
blue. The rest are red.
How many red blocks
does Maria have?

_____ – _____ = _____

_____ red blocks

3 10 turtles are at the beach.
3 are green. The rest are brown.
How many turtles are brown?

_____ – _____ = _____

_____ brown turtles

Subtract. Write the difference.

4 6 – 3 = _____

5 _____ = 8 – 1

6
  9
– 6
☐

7
  10
– 7
☐

8
  7
– 5
☐

9
  8
– 4
☐

Test Prep

Fill in the bubble next to the correct answer.

10 6 bunnies are in the grass.
Then 2 bunnies hop away.

Which equation shows how many
bunnies are in the grass now?

○ $6 - 5 = 1$

○ $6 - 2 = 4$

○ $8 - 2 = 6$

Subtract. Write the difference.

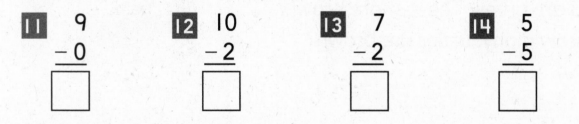

11   9
        $- 0$

12   10
        $- 2$

13   7
        $- 2$

14   5
        $- 5$

Spiral Review

Solve.

15 Use a doubles fact to add $4 + 5$.

$4 + 4 =$ _____

So, $4 + 5 =$ _____ .

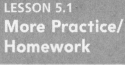

Represent Result Unknown Problems with Objects and Drawings

(MP) **Model with Mathematics Solve.**
Draw to show your thinking.

1 Ellen has 8 shells. Danielle gives
her 5 more shells. How many
shells does Ellen have now?

Equation: _____

Ellen has _____ shells.

2 There are 17 geese in a pond.
Then 8 geese fly away. How
many geese are still in the pond?

Equation: _____

_____ geese are still in the pond.

3 Brynn finds 9 acorns on a hike.
She finds 6 more. How many
acorns does she have now?

Equation: _____

Brynn has _____ acorns.

Solve.

4 $9 + 9 =$ _____ | **5** $7 + 8 =$ _____

Test Prep

Fill in the bubble next to the correct answer.

6 There are 13 peaches in a basket. Linda takes 7 peaches. How many peaches are in the basket now?

○ 9   ○ 7   ○ 6

7 Luca eats 6 grapes from a bowl. Then he eats 5 more grapes. How many grapes does he eat?

○ 12   ○ 11   ○ 1

Spiral Review

Add.

8 $3 + 3 = \underline{\hspace{2em}}$ **9** $6 + 6 = \underline{\hspace{2em}}$ **10** $7 + 7 = \underline{\hspace{2em}}$

Write the sum. Change the order of the addends. Add again.

11 $5 + 4 = \underline{\hspace{2em}}$ $\underline{\hspace{2em}} + \underline{\hspace{2em}} = \underline{\hspace{2em}}$

12 $8 + 5 = \underline{\hspace{2em}}$ $\underline{\hspace{2em}} + \underline{\hspace{2em}} = \underline{\hspace{2em}}$

13 $3 + 9 = \underline{\hspace{2em}}$ $\underline{\hspace{2em}} + \underline{\hspace{2em}} = \underline{\hspace{2em}}$

Name _____

LESSON 5.2
More Practice/ Homework

ONLINE
Video Tutorials and
Interactive Examples

Represent Change Unknown Problems with Objects and Drawings

Solve. Draw to show your thinking.

1 **MP Reason** There are 8 bees in a flower garden. Some more bees come. Now there are 12 bees. How many bees come to the garden?

_____ bees

2 Kaleb has 12 leaves. He loses some of the leaves. He has 9 leaves now. How many leaves does he lose?

Equation: _____ _____ leaves

3 **MP Model with Mathematics** Valerie has 16 marbles. She gives some to a friend. Now she has 7 marbles. How many marbles does she give to a friend?

Equation: _____ _____ marbles

4 14 − _____ = 7

5 3 + _____ = 11

Test Prep

Fill in the bubble next to the correct answer.

6 There are 13 pears in a bowl. Trina
takes some pears. There are 6 pears left.
How many pears does Trina take?

   ○ 12   ○ 7   ○ 4

7 Oscar has 5 cups. He gets some more cups.
Now he has 11 cups. How many more cups
does he get?

   ○ 11   ○ 7   ○ 6

Spiral Review

**Solve two ways. Circle the addends you
add first.**

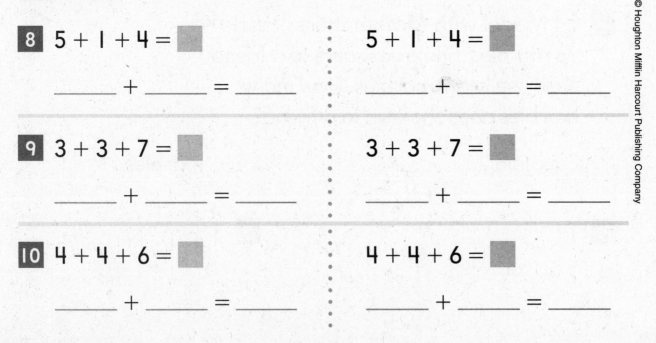

8 $5 + 1 + 4 = \boxed{}$

_____ + _____ = _____

$5 + 1 + 4 = \boxed{}$

_____ + _____ = _____

9 $3 + 3 + 7 = \boxed{}$

_____ + _____ = _____

$3 + 3 + 7 = \boxed{}$

_____ + _____ = _____

10 $4 + 4 + 6 = \boxed{}$

_____ + _____ = _____

$4 + 4 + 6 = \boxed{}$

_____ + _____ = _____

Name _____

Represent Start Unknown Problems with Objects and Drawings

Solve. Draw or write to show your thinking.

1 (MP) **Reason** Cora draws some pictures. She gives 5 pictures away. She has 8 pictures left. How many pictures did she draw to start?

_____ pictures

2 (MP) **Model with Mathematics** Lindsay makes some rings. Then she makes 5 more rings. Now she has 11 rings. How many rings did she make to start?

Equation: _____

_____ rings

3 **Open Ended** Write a story problem for this equation. Solve the problem.

▇ $+ 9 = 16$

_____

_____

Add or subtract.

4 _____ $+ 7 = 16$ **5** _____ $- 8 = 6$ **6** _____ $+ 9 = 15$

Test Prep

Fill in the bubble next to the correct answer.

7 Some oranges are in a bowl. Maddie puts 7 more oranges in the bowl. Now there are 12 oranges in the bowl. How many oranges were in the bowl to start?

○ 5   ○ 7   ○ 12

8 Brody has some sheets of paper. He gives 9 sheets of paper to a friend. He has 9 sheets of paper left. How many sheets of paper did he have to start?

○ 12   ○ 15   ○ 18

Spiral Review

Write an addition equation to help you solve.

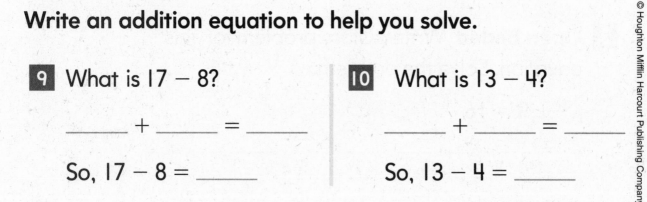

9 What is 17 − 8?

_____ + _____ = _____

So, 17 − 8 = _____

10 What is 13 − 4?

_____ + _____ = _____

So, 13 − 4 = _____

Name _____

Solve Add To and Take From Problems

(MP) **Model with Mathematics** Solve.
Draw to show your work.

1 Joe puts 5 slices of cheese on a plate.
Then he puts more slices of cheese on the
plate. Now there are 12 slices of cheese.
How many more slices of cheese
does Joe put on the plate?

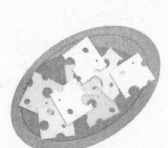

Equation: _____

_____ slices of cheese

---

2 Ivy has 8 beads. She gets 9 more
beads. How many beads does
she have now?

Equation: _____

_____ beads

---

3 Antonio has 14 puppets. He gives
some to Ivan. Now Antonio has
6 puppets. How many does he
give to Ivan?

Equation: _____

_____ puppets

Test Prep

Fill in the bubble next to the correct answer.

4 Jack has some bananas. He gives 7 bananas to Erin. Now he has 4 bananas. How many bananas did he have to start?

Which equation solves the problem?

○ $7 - 4 = 3$ ○ $7 + 4 = 11$ ○ $7 + 7 = 14$

5 Alexa has 4 apples. Randy gives her some more apples. Now she has 12 apples. How many apples does Randy give Alexa?

○ 4   ○ 6   ○ 8

Spiral Review

Add to subtract.

6 Rick sees 9 baseballs. 4 baseballs are in a bag and the rest are on the grass. How many baseballs are on the grass?

$9 - 4 = $ ▢

$4 + \underline{\quad} = 9$

So, $9 - 4 = \underline{\quad}$

\underline{\quad} baseballs

© Houghton Mifflin Harcourt Publishing Company

Name _____

Represent Total Unknown Problems with Objects and Drawings

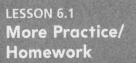

ONLINE
Video Tutorials and Interactive Examples

Write an equation to solve.

1 (MP) **Model with Mathematics** There are 8 seahorses and 8 fish in the water. How many seahorses and fish are there in all? Draw to show your thinking.

Equation: _____

_____ seahorses and fish

2 8 children play on the swings and 4 children play on the slide. How many children play on the swings and slide?

Equation: _____

_____ children.

Add.

3 $9 + 6 =$ _____

4 $7 + 7 =$ _____

5 $4 + 7 =$ _____

6 $5 + 8 =$ _____

Test Prep

Fill in the bubble next to the correct answer.

7 Ricardo has 7 baseball cards. Zoe has 5 baseball cards. How many baseball cards do they have altogether?

○ 2 baseball cards

○ 12 baseball cards

○ 15 baseball cards

8 There are 8 blue crabs and 6 red crabs sitting in the sand. How many crabs are there?

○ 10 crabs

○ 12 crabs

○ 14 crabs

Spiral Review

Add. Write the doubles fact you used to solve the problem.

9 $5 + 6 =$ _____

_____ + _____ = _____

10 $8 + 7 =$ _____

_____ + _____ = _____

Solve two ways. Circle the addends you add first.

11 $5 + 4 + 4 =$ ▮

_____ + _____ = _____

12 $5 + 4 + 4 =$ ▮

_____ + _____ = _____

Represent Both Addends Unknown Problems with Objects and Drawings

Open Ended Draw to show your thinking. Write an equation to solve.

1 There are 16 bananas and apples in a bowl. How many of each could there be?

Equation: _____

_____ bananas and _____ apples

2 There are 14 dogs in the park. Some are brown and some are white. How many of each could there be?

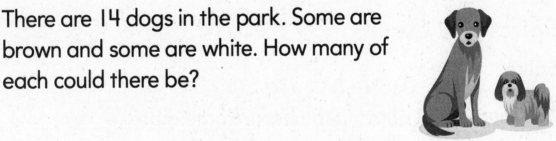

Equation: _____

_____ brown dogs and _____ white dogs

Test Prep

Fill in the bubble next to the correct answer.

3 A baseball team has 13 baseball bats.
Some are wood and some are metal.
How many of each could they have?

○ 9 metal bats and 3 wood bats

○ 7 metal bats and 5 wood bats

○ 6 metal bats and 7 wood bats

4 Jody has 12 toy animals. She has elephants
and tigers. How many of each could she have?

○ 3 elephants and 9 tigers

○ 5 elephants and 9 tigers

○ 8 elephants and 5 tigers

Spiral Review

Solve.

5 There are 2 goats in the barn. Some more
goats come. Now there are 11 goats in the
barn. How many goats come in the barn?

Equation: _____

_____ goats

6 $7 + \_\_\_\_ = 10$

7 $16 - \_\_\_\_ = 9$

Represent Addend Unknown Problems with Objects and Drawings

Draw to show your thinking. Write an equation to solve.

1. (MP) **Model with Mathematics** There are 13 kittens. 5 are sleeping and the rest are playing. How many kittens are playing?

   Equation: _____

   There are _____ kittens playing.

Write an equation to solve.

2. Talie sees 12 cats and dogs. There are 5 dogs and the rest are cats. How many cats does she see?

   Equation: _____

   _____ cats

Solve.

3. $17 = 8 + \underline{\hspace{1cm}}$

4. $16 = \underline{\hspace{1cm}} + 9$

5. $6 + \underline{\hspace{1cm}} = 11$

6. $9 + \underline{\hspace{1cm}} = 15$

Test Prep

Fill in the bubble next to the correct answer.

7 There are 15 bugs. 7 are butterflies and the rest are bees. How many bees are there?

○ 7 bees

○ 8 bees

○ 11 bees

8 Carlos has 14 strawberries and grapes. He has 8 strawberries and the rest are grapes. How many grapes are there? Which equation solves the problem?

○ $14 = 8 + 6$

○ $14 = 7 + 7$

○ $14 = 5 + 9$

Spiral Review

Subtract. Then add to check your answer.

9 $8 - 5 =$ _____

_____ + _____ = _____

10 $17 - 9 =$ _____

_____ + _____ = _____

Represent Total Unknown Problems with a Visual Model

Use a bar model to solve the problem.

1 Matthew sees 9 plants with white flowers and 8 plants with pink flowers in a garden. How many plants does he see?

_____	_____

_____

Equation: _____

Matthew sees _____ plants.

2 **Open Ended** Complete the bar model. Write a story problem to match the bar model.

8	4

_____

_____

_____

_____

Test Prep

Use a bar model to solve the problem.

3 Jasmine has 7 toy lions and 6 toy tigers. How many toy lions and tigers does Jasmine have in all? Use a bar model to solve the problem.

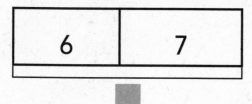

6	7

Jasmine has _____ toy lions and tigers.

---

4 Use the bar model. Fill in the bubble of the equation that describes the problem.

3	8

11

○ $8 - 3 = 5$ ○ $3 + 8 = 11$ ○ $9 + 3 = 12$

Spiral Review

Solve two ways. Circle to group the two addends you will add first.

5 $6 + 2 + 4 =$ ▢

_____ + _____ = _____

So $6 + 2 + 4 =$ _____

Name _____

LESSON 6.5
More Practice/ Homework

ONLINE
Video Tutorials and
Interactive Examples

Represent Addend Unknown and Both Addends Unknown Problems with a Visual Model

Use a bar model to solve.

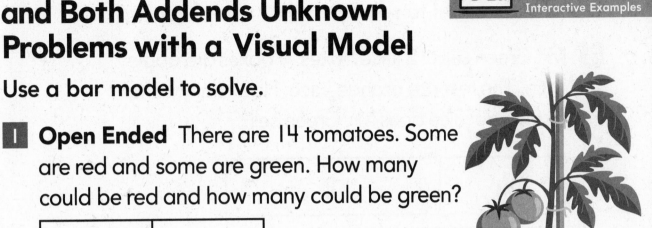

1 **Open Ended** There are 14 tomatoes. Some are red and some are green. How many could be red and how many could be green?

```
┌──────────┬──────────┐
│          │          │
│  _____  │  _____  │
└──────────┴──────────┘
```

_____

Equation: _____

_____ red tomatoes _____ green tomatoes

---

2 **MP Model with Mathematics** There are 16 ducks. Some are in the pond. 7 are on the grass. How many ducks are in the pond?

```
┌──────────┬──────────┐
│          │          │
│  _____  │  _____  │
└──────────┴──────────┘
```

_____

Equation: _____

_____ ducks are in the pond.

Test Prep

Use a bar model to solve.

3 Mr. Green sells 12 juice boxes. 4 boxes are apple juice. The rest are orange juice. How many boxes of orange juice does Mr. Green sell?

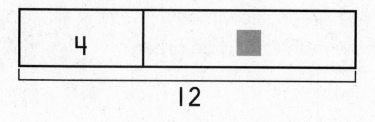

_____ boxes of orange juice

4 Mrs. Wong has 11 pencils and pens. How many can be pencils and how many can be pens? Fill in the bubble of the equation that solves the problem.

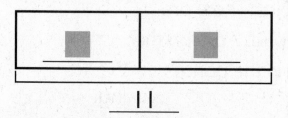

○ 6 − 5 = 1   ○ 5 + 6 = 11   ○ 6 + 7 = 13

Spiral Review

Subtract.

5 15 − 9 = _____   **6** 13 − 8 = _____

7 16 − 7 = _____   **8** 14 − 6 = _____

Name _____

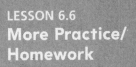
ONLINE
Video Tutorials and
Interactive Examples

Solve Put Together and Take Apart Problems

Solve.

1 (MP) **Use Repeated Reasoning** There are
12 pieces of fruit in a bowl. Some are plums
and some are peaches. How many could
be plums and how many could be peaches?
Complete the bar model and write an equation.

Equation: _____

_____ plums _____ peaches

---

2 (MP) **Reason** A bakery sells 15 muffins. 9 are
blueberry and the rest are apple. How many
muffins are apple? Draw to show your thinking.

Equation: _____

_____ muffins.

Module 6 • Lesson 6

Test Prep

Use a bar model to solve.

3 There are 17 cups on a table. 9 are red and the rest are blue. How many blue cups are there?

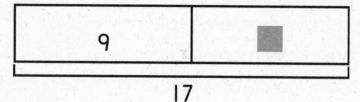

_____ blue cups

4 A soccer team has 9 white soccer balls and 3 green soccer balls. How many soccer balls does the team have? Fill in the bubble of the equation that solves the problem.

○ $9 - 3 = 6$

○ $12 = 4 + 8$

○ $9 + 3 = 12$

Spiral Review

Use subtraction to find the unknown addend.

5 Solve $9 +$ ▢ $= 15$

_____ − _____ = _____

$9 +$ _____ $= 15$

6 Solve $8 +$ ▢ $= 14$

_____ − _____ = _____

$8 +$ _____ $= 14$

Name _____

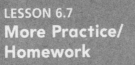
Solve Addition and Subtraction Problems

Use a bar model and write an equation to solve.

1 David has some pinecones. He gives 9 to Aaron. He has 7 left. How many pinecones did David start with?

```
┌─────────────────┬─────────────────┐
│                 │                 │
│     _____     │     _____     │
└─────────────────┴─────────────────┘
```

_____

Equation: _____

David started with _____ pinecones.

Write an equation to solve.

2 **Open Ended** The Beach Shop has 15 sand pails. The pails are red or blue. How many of each color could there be?

Equation: _____

_____ red sand pails   _____ blue sand pails

Add or subtract.

3 $8 + 5 =$ _____ | **4** $16 -$ _____ $= 8$ | **5** $7 + 5 =$ _____

© Houghton Mifflin Harcourt Publishing Company

Test Prep

Fill in the bubble next to the correct answer.

6 Annabelle has some smiley face stickers. She gives 4 stickers to Luke. She has 9 stickers left. Which equation can you use to find how many stickers she started with?

○ $9 - 4 = 5$ ○ $9 + 4 = 13$ ○ $4 + 5 = 9$

7 Rick has 12 stickers. He gives some to Lucy. Now he has 9 stickers. How many stickers does he give to Lucy?

○ 3 stickers   ○ 6 stickers   ○ 9 stickers

8 Asa has 7 star stickers. Miguel gives her 6 more stickers. How many stickers does Asa have altogether?

○ 15 stickers   ○ 14 stickers   ○ 13 stickers

Spiral Review

Write a related subtraction fact to solve.

9 6 horses are in the barn. Some more horses come. Now there are 11 horses. How many horses come to the barn?

_____ – _____ = _____

$6 +$ _____ $= 11$ _____ horses

© Houghton Mifflin Harcourt Publishing Company

LESSON 7.1
**More Practice/
Homework**

ONLINE
Video Tutorials and
Interactive Examples

Represent Difference Unknown Problems with Objects and Drawings

(MP) **Model with Mathematics** Draw counters and write an equation.

1 Eric has 7 fish. Nancy has 9 fish. How many more fish does Nancy have than Eric?

Equation: _____

Nancy has _____ more fish than Eric.

2 There are 5 red counters and 7 green counters. How many fewer red counters are there than green counters?

Equation: _____

There are _____ fewer red counters.

© Houghton Mifflin Harcourt Publishing Company

Test Prep

Fill in the bubble next to the correct answer.

3 There are 3 red counters. There are 6 green counters. How many fewer red counters are there than green counters?

○ 2 fewer red counters

○ 3 fewer red counters

○ 9 fewer red counters

4 There are 5 red counters. There are 8 green counters. How many more green counters are there than red counters?

Which equation models the problem?

○ $8 - 5 = 3$

○ $8 + 3 = 11$

○ $5 + 8 = 13$

Spiral Review

5 Carlos has 7 baseball cards. He gives 2 to his friend. How many cards does Carlos have now?

Write a subtraction equation to model the problem.

_____ − _____ = _____

Carlos has _____ baseball cards now.

Represent Bigger Unknown Problems with Objects and Drawings

 Model with Mathematics Draw counters and write an equation.

1 Celeste has 7 plastic bottles to recycle. Muriel has 2 more than Celeste. How many plastic bottles does Muriel have?

Equation: _____

Muriel has _____ plastic bottles.

---

2 Open Ended Explain how you know how many fewer circles there are than triangles.

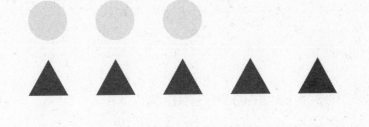

_____

_____

_____

Test Prep

Fill in the bubble next to the correct answer.

3 Alicia has 3 toy pandas. Traci has 7 more toy pandas than Alicia. How many toy pandas does Traci have?

○ 10 pandas   ○ 4 pandas   ○ 3 pandas

4 Otto has 3 more books than Zahra. Zahra has 8 books. How many books does Otto have?

○ 3 books   ○ 5 books   ○ 11 books

Spiral Review

Draw to show your thinking. Write an equation to solve.

5 There are 16 vegetables. There are 9 ears of corn and the rest are peppers. How many are peppers?

Equation: _____

There are _____ peppers.

6 Sahil has 13 paper plates. He gives some to James. Now Sahil has 8 paper plates. How many paper plates does Sahil give to James?

Equation: _____

Sahil gives _____ paper plates to James.

LESSON 7.3
**More Practice/
Homework**

 ONLINE
Video Tutorials and
Interactive Examples

Represent Smaller Unknown Problems with Objects and Drawings

(MP) **Model with Mathematics** Draw counters.
Write an equation.

1 Gerry has 10 grapes. Theresa has
3 fewer grapes than Gerry. How
many grapes does Theresa have?

Equation: _____

Theresa has _____ grapes.

2 Ming draws 2 more squares than
Abe. Ming draws 7 squares.
How many squares does Abe draw?

Equation: _____

Abe draws _____ squares.

3 **Open Ended** Brian compares the
number of triangles to circles. Write an
equation that compares the shapes.

_____

Test Prep

Fill in the bubble next to the correct answer.

4 Grace has 8 roses. Esther has
3 fewer roses than Grace.
How many roses does Esther have?

○ 8 roses

○ 6 roses

○ 5 roses

5 Lizzy has 10 toy animals. Maribel has
2 fewer toy animals than Lizzy. How
many toy animals does Maribel have?

Which equation models the problem?

○ $10 + 2 = 12$

○ $10 - 2 = 8$

○ $7 + 2 = 9$

Spiral Review

Use a bar model to solve.

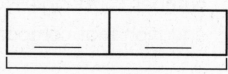

6 Ahmad has 15 cubes. Some are
red and some are blue. How many
red and blue cubes could there be?

_____ red cubes   _____ blue cubes

LESSON 7.4
**More Practice/
Homework**

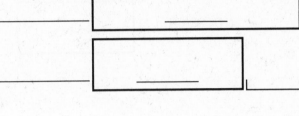

ONLINE
Video Tutorials and
Interactive Examples

Represent Difference Unknown Problems with a Visual Model

(MP) **Model with Mathematics** Complete the bar model. Write an equation.

1 Mr. Royce buys 11 pears. He buys 8 plums. How many more pears does he buy than plums?

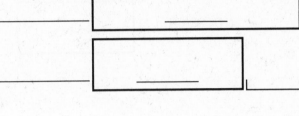

Equation: _____

Mr. Royce buys _____ more pears than plums.

2 **Math on the Spot** Pam has 2 marbles. Rick has 9 marbles. How many fewer marbles does Pam have than Rick?

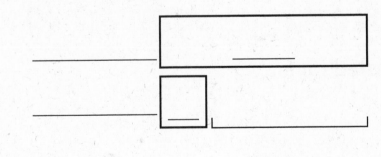

Equation: _____

Pam has _____ fewer marbles than Rick.

Test Prep

Fill in the bubble next to the correct answer.

3 There are 16 goldfish in a fish tank. There are 9 rocks in the tank. How many fewer rocks are there than goldfish?

○ 7 fewer rocks

○ 8 fewer rocks

○ 9 fewer rocks

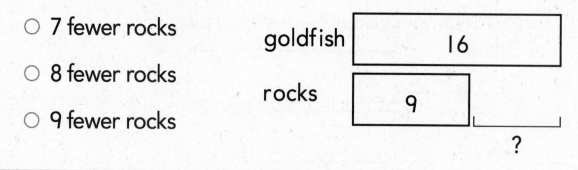

4 Fill in the bubble next to the equation that describes the bar model shown.

○ 8 + 9 = 17

○ 16 − 8 = 8

○ 10 + 7 = 17

Spiral Review

Complete the related facts.

5 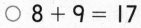 13 − 7 = _____   13 − 6 = _____

7 + _____ = 13   6 + _____ = 13

LESSON 7.5
**More Practice/
Homework**

 ONLINE
Video Tutorials and
Interactive Examples

Represent Bigger Unknown and Smaller Unknown Problems with a Visual Model

(MP) **Model with Mathematics** Complete the bar model. Write an equation.

1 Anton has 8 books. Cybil has 4 more books than Anton. How many books does Cybil have?

Equation: _____

Cybil has _____ books.

2 There are 10 green apples in a basket. There are 5 fewer red apples in the basket. How many red apples are there?

Equation: _____

There are _____ red apples.

3 Sully wins 6 games. He wins 7 fewer games than Robin. How many games does Robin win?

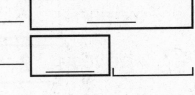

Equation: _____

Robin wins _____ games.

Test Prep

Fill in the bubble next to the correct answer.

4 There are 7 blue counters. There are 8 more red counters than blue counters. How many red counters are there?

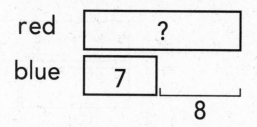

red | ? |
blue | 7 |
8

○ 13 red counters ○ 15 red counters ○ 18 red counters

5 Leo counts 16 pigeons at the park. He counts 9 fewer doves. How many doves does Leo count?

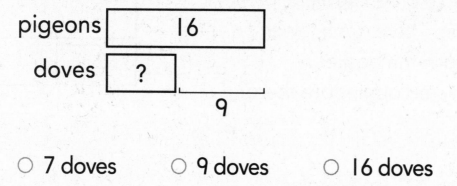

pigeons | 16 |
doves | ? |
9

○ 7 doves ○ 9 doves ○ 16 doves

Spiral Review

Use subtraction to find the unknown addend.

6 Solve 5 + ▨ = 13.

_____ − _____ = _____

5 + _____ = 13

Name _____

Use Strategies to Solve Compare Problems

1  **Use Repeated Reasoning** Sheila sees 12 starfish. Nicole sees 6 fewer starfish than Sheila. How many starfish does Nicole see?

Choose a strategy to solve the problem.

Add Doubles   **Make a Ten**

Draw or write to show the strategy.

Nicole sees _____ starfish.

2 Mike counts 7 buses in the parking lot. He counts 6 more vans than buses in the lot. How many vans are in the parking lot?

Use a strategy to solve the problem.

Draw or write to show the strategy.

There are _____ vans in the parking lot.

Test Prep

Fill in the bubble next to the correct answer.

3 Madison finds 6 rocks on the beach. Avana finds 8 more rocks than Madison. How many rocks does Avana find?

○ 2 rocks   ○ 13 rocks   ○ 14 rocks

4 There are 7 red marbles. There are 11 blue marbles. How many fewer red marbles are there than blue marbles?

○ 4 fewer marbles   ○ 7 fewer marbles   ○ 18 fewer marbles

Spiral Review

Make a ten to subtract. Draw counters to show your work.

5 There are 13 paper hearts in the box. 8 are pink. The rest are green. How many paper hearts are green?

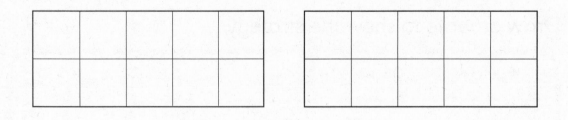

_____ − _____ = _____

_____ green paper hearts

Name _____

LESSON 7.7
More Practice/ Homework

ONLINE
Video Tutorials and
Interactive Examples

Solve Addition and Subtraction Situations

Show how to solve the problem. Write an equation and the answer.

1 Randy picks 7 roses. Sherri picks 9 more roses than Randy. How many roses does Sherri pick?

Equation: _____

Sherri picks _____ roses.

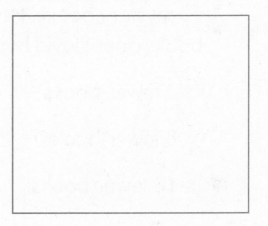

2 Chen has 12 pencils. He gives some to his friend. Now Chen has 7 pencils. How many pencils does Chen give to his friend?

Equation: _____

Chen gives _____ pencils to his friend.

3 Sophie has 8 barrettes. Judy has 12 barrettes. How many more barrettes does Judy have than Sophie?

Equation: _____

Judy has _____ more barrettes than Sophie.

Test Prep

Fill in the bubble next to the correct answer.

4 Christian has 9 postcards. Joy has 3 more postcards than Christian. How many postcards does Joy have?

○ 6 postcards

○ 12 postcards

○ 15 postcards

5 David has 8 mystery books. Saxon has 10 mystery books. How many fewer mystery books does David have than Saxon?

○ 2 fewer books

○ 8 fewer books

○ 18 fewer books

Spiral Review

Complete the bar model. Write an equation.

6 Kenji has 4 buttons. Finn has 12 buttons. How many fewer buttons does Kenji have than Finn?

Equation: _____

Kenji has _____ fewer buttons.

© Houghton Mifflin Harcourt Publishing Company

Interpret Picture Graphs

Use the picture graph to answer the questions.

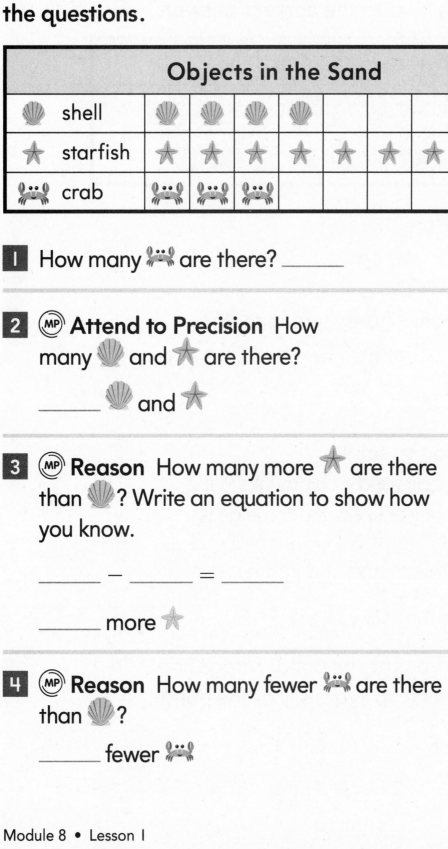

Objects in the Sand									
🐚 shell	🐚	🐚	🐚	🐚					
⭐ starfish	⭐	⭐	⭐	⭐	⭐	⭐	⭐	⭐	⭐
🦀 crab	🦀	🦀	🦀						

1 How many 🦀 are there? _____

2 (MP) **Attend to Precision** How many 🐚 and ⭐ are there?

_____ 🐚 and ⭐

3 (MP) **Reason** How many more ⭐ are there than 🐚? Write an equation to show how you know.

_____ − _____ = _____

_____ more ⭐

4 (MP) **Reason** How many fewer 🦀 are there than 🐚?

_____ fewer 🦀

Test Prep

Use the picture graph to answer the questions.
Fill in the bubble next to the correct answer.

Flowers in the Garden											
☀ daisy	☀	☀	☀	☀	☀	☀	☀	☀	☀	☀	
🌷 tulip	🌷	🌷	🌷	🌷	🌷	🌷	🌷	🌷			

5 How many 🌷 are there?

    ○ 18   ○ 10   ○ 8

6 How many more ☀ are there than 🌷?

    ○ 2 more   ○ 8 more   ○ 10 more

Spiral Review

Write an equation to solve.

7 There are 7 rabbits and 6 chipmunks in the grass. How many animals are in the grass?

Equation: _____

_____ animals

8 There are 11 frogs at the pond. 7 frogs hop away. How many frogs are still at the pond?

Equation: _____

_____ frogs

LESSON 8.2
**More Practice/
Homework**

ONLINE
Video Tutorials and
Interactive Examples

Represent Data with Picture Graphs

1 (MP) **Use Tools** Ray has 3 circles, 4 triangles, and 5 squares. Make a picture graph to show his shapes.

Shapes Ray Has								
⬛ square								
⬤ circle								
🔺 triangle								

Use your picture graph to answer the questions.

2 How many circles and triangles are there?

_____ circles and triangles

3 (MP) **Attend to Precision** Are there more squares or triangles?

_____

How many more? _____ more

4 (MP) **Attend to Precision** Are there fewer circles or squares?

_____

How many fewer? _____ fewer

Test Prep

Fill in the bubble next to the correct answer.

Animals in the Animal Park								
🦓 zebra	🦓	🦓	🦓	🦓	🦓	🦓		
🦒 giraffe	🦒	🦒	🦒	🦒	🦒			
🦛 hippo	🦛	🦛	🦛					

5 How many 🦓 are there?

○ 3   ○ 6   ○ 19

6 How many more 🦒 are there than 🦛 ?

○ 5 more   ○ 3 more   ○ 2 more

Spiral Review

Add or subtract.

7 10
     − 3

8   1
     + 4

9   8
     − 8

10 8
     + 1

11 9
     + 1

12 2
     + 6

13 5
     − 4

14 7
     − 3

Name _____

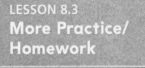
Interpret Tally Charts

1  **Attend to Precision** Complete the tally chart.

Toys on the Shelf		Total
🚌 bus	l	
🚗 car	卌 lll	
🚚 truck	卌 l	

Use the tally chart to answer the questions.

2 How many 🚗 are there?

_____ 🚗

3 How many 🚚 and 🚚 are there?

_____ 🚚 and 🚚

4 🅜🅟 **Attend to Precision**
How many fewer 🚚 are there than 🚗 ?

_____ fewer

5 🅜🅟 **Attend to Precision**
How many more 🚗 are there than 🚚 ?

_____ more

Test Prep

Bugs in the Grass		Total
🐞	⊞⊞⊞	5
🐜	⊞⊞⊞ I	6
🐛	III	3

Use the tally chart to answer the questions.
Fill in the bubble next to the correct answer.

6 How many 🐞 and 🐜 are there?

   ○ 5   ○ 10   ○ 11

7 How many more 🐞 are there than 🐛?

   ○ 2 more   ○ 3 more   ○ 5 more

Spiral Review

Write an equation to solve.

8 There are 12 frogs at the pond. 3 frogs are brown.
The rest are green. How many frogs are green?

Equation: _____

_____ green frogs

LESSON 8.4
**More Practice/
Homework**

@Ed **ONLINE**
Video Tutorials and
Interactive Examples

Represent Data with Tally Charts

1 (MP) **Attend to Precision** Use the picture to make a tally chart.

Sports Balls Jo Has		Total
🔘 golf ball		
🎾 tennis ball		

2 How many sports balls does Jo have?

_____ sports balls

3 (MP) **Reason** Are there more golf balls or tennis balls?

_____

How many more?
_____ more

4 Use the picture to make a tally chart.

Fish in the Bowl		Total
🐟		
🐟		
🐟		

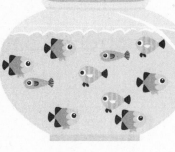

5 (MP) **Attend to Precision** How many fewer 🐟 are there than 🐟?   _____ fewer 🐟

Test Prep

Balloons at the Park			Total
plain		IIII	4
dotted		ЖНТ II	7
striped		I	I

Use the tally chart to answer the questions.
Fill in the bubble next to the correct answer.

6 How many balloons are there?

○ 4   ○ II   ○ 12

7 How many more ● are there than ●?

○ I more   ○ 6 more   ○ 7 more

Spiral Review

Subtract. Complete the related facts.

8 $11 - 6 =$ _____   _____ $+$ _____ $=$ _____

_____ $-$ _____ $=$ _____   _____ $+$ _____ $=$ _____

Name _____

LESSON 8.5
**More Practice/
Homework**

ONLINE
Video Tutorials and
Interactive Examples

Interpret Bar Graphs

Some children were asked which activity
they like best.

(MP) **Attend to Precision** Use the bar graph to
answer the questions.

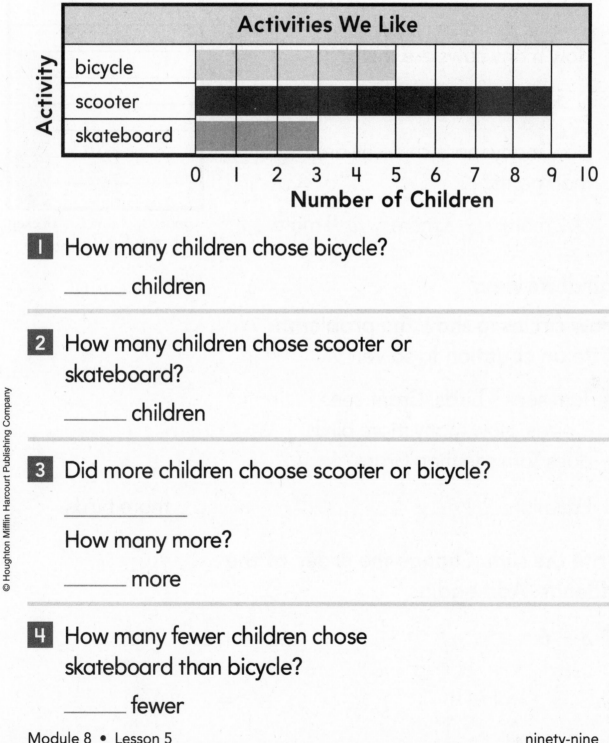

1 How many children chose bicycle?

_____ children

2 How many children chose scooter or
skateboard?

_____ children

3 Did more children choose scooter or bicycle?

_____

How many more?

_____ more

4 How many fewer children chose
skateboard than bicycle?

_____ fewer

© Houghton Mifflin Harcourt Publishing Company

Test Prep

Use the bar graph to answer the questions.

5 How many animals are on
the farm?

○ 4   ○ 7   ○ 13

6 How many cows are there?

○ 3   ○ 4   ○ 6

7 How many more chickens are there
than goats?

○ 2 more   ○ 3 more   ○ 4 more

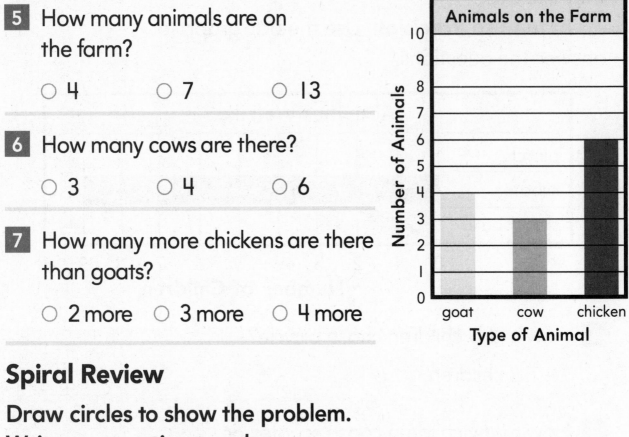

Spiral Review

Draw circles to show the problem.
Write an equation to solve.

8 Tam sees 8 birds. Grant sees
3 birds. How many more birds
does Tam see than Grant?

Equation: _____   _____ more birds

Write the sum. Change the order of the
addends. Add again.

9 $3 + 6 =$ _____   _____ + _____ = _____

10 _____ $= 1 + 4$ _____ $=$ _____ + _____

Name _____

Represent Data with Bar Graphs

1 (MP) **Attend to Precision** Make a bar graph to show the following data.

Some children wore caps to school today.

- 3 gray caps

- 4 white caps

- 1 black cap

Use your bar graph to answer the questions.

2 How many caps were worn today?

_____ caps

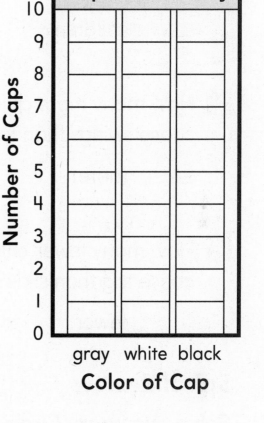

3 (MP) **Model with Mathematics** How many more children would need to wear black caps to have the same number as white caps? Write an equation to explain.

Equation: _____

_____ children

Test Prep

Use the bar graph to answer the questions.

4 How many children chose swings or slide?

_____ children

5 How many more children chose swings than tag?

_____ more

6 How many fewer children chose tag than slide?

_____ fewer

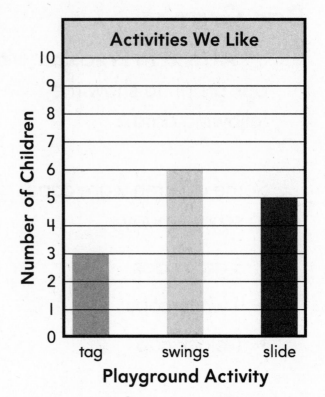

Spiral Review

Solve two ways. Circle the addends you add first.

7 $3 + 4 + 1 = $ ▢

_____ + _____ = _____

$3 + 4 + 1 = $ ▢

_____ + _____ = _____

8 $2 + 3 + 4 = $ ▢

_____ + _____ = _____

$2 + 3 + 4 = $ ▢

_____ + _____ = _____

Using Data to Solve Problems

1 (MP) **Attend to Precision** Make a bar graph to show the problem. Then use the graph to solve the problem.

There are 15 pieces of fruit in a bowl. There are 4 bananas. There are 2 more plums than bananas. The rest are apples. How many apples are there?

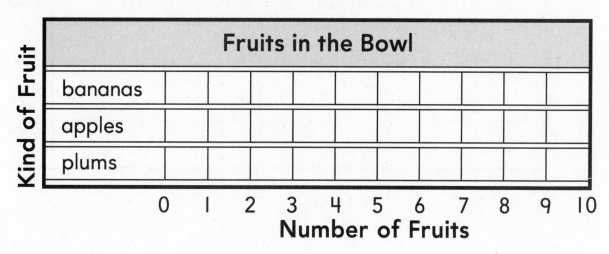

Kind of Fruit

Fruits in the Bowl

bananas										
apples										
plums										

0   1   2   3   4   5   6   7   8   9   10

Number of Fruits

There are _____ apples.

2 (MP) **Construct Arguments** Explain how you found the number of apples.

_____

_____

_____

Test Prep

3 The tally chart shows the problem.
Use the tally chart to solve the problem.

There are 3 paintbrushes in the classroom. There are 5 more crayons than paintbrushes. There are 4 fewer markers than crayons. How many markers are there?

Art Supplies in the Classroom		Total
paintbrush	III	3
crayon	卌 III	8
marker	▢	▢

There are _____ markers.

Spiral Review

Write an equation to solve.

4 There are 4 bunnies. 8 bunnies join them. How many bunnies are there now?

Equation: _____

_____ bunnies

Add or subtract.

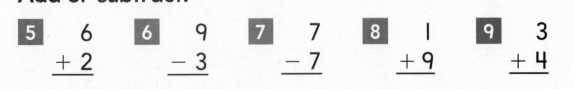

5	6	**6**	9	**7**	7	**8**	1	**9**	3
	+2		−3		−7		+9		+4

© Houghton Mifflin Harcourt Publishing Company

LESSON 9.1
**More Practice/
Homework**

ONLINE
Video Tutorials and
Interactive Examples

Make Ten and Ones

(MP) Use Structure Solve. Draw a
quick picture to show the number.

1 Coach Alex has 8 baseballs. Then he gets
3 more baseballs. How many baseballs
does Coach Alex have now?

_____ baseballs

2 Keenan sees 9 ducks and 6 turtles at the
pond. How many animals does he see?

_____ animals

3 Gina helps at the library. She puts 7 books
on a shelf. Then she puts 7 more books on
the shelf. How many books does Gina put
on the shelf?

_____ books

Write the number shown by the quick picture.

4
○
○
○

_____

5
○
○
○ ○
○ ○
○ ○

_____

Test Prep

Which number is shown by the quick picture?
Fill in the bubble next to the correct answer.

6

- ○ 15
- ○ 10
- ○ 5

7

- ○ 12
- ○ 17
- ○ 18

Spiral Review

Solve.

8 There are 6 birds in a tree and 5 birds on the ground. How many birds are there? Write an equation to solve the problem.

Equation: _____

_____ birds

9 There are 12 flowers in a vase. Some are red and some are pink. How many of each color flower could there be?

_____ red flowers and _____ pink flowers

Understand Ten and Ones

Write the number three ways to solve.

1 **(MP) Use Structure** Callie has 10 goldfish.
She gets 9 more goldfish. How many goldfish
does Callie have now? Draw to show your
thinking.

_____ + _____

_____ ten _____ ones

_____ goldfish

2 **Math on the Spot** Karen has 7 ones.
Jimmy has 8 ones. They put all of their ones
together. What number did they make?

_____ + _____

_____ ten _____ ones

_____

Write the number three ways.

3

_____ + _____

_____ ten _____ ones

_____

Test Prep

Fill in the bubble next to the correct answer.

4 Which is a way to write the number?

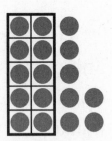

   ○ I ten 7 ones   ○ I ten 5 ones   ○ I ten 2 ones

5 Which is a way to write the number?

   ○ I + 5   ○ 10 + 3   ○ 10 + 5

Spiral Review

Make a tally chart to show the problem.
Then use the tally chart to solve the problem.

6 There are red, blue, and green marbles in a
bag. 4 marbles are red. The same number
of marbles are blue. There are 15 marbles
in all. How many green marbles are there?

Marbles in the Bag	Total
red	
blue	
green	

_____ green marbles

Name _____

LESSON 9.3
**More Practice/
Homework**

ONLINE
Video Tutorials and
Interactive Examples

Make Tens

 Attend to Precision Draw a
quick picture to solve.

1 Mrs. Potter has 6 boxes of pencils. There are
10 pencils in each box. How many pencils
does Mrs. Potter have?

_____ tens _____ ones = _____

_____ pencils

2 There are 3 rows of desks in a classroom.
There are 10 desks in each row. How many
desks are there?

_____ tens _____ ones = _____

_____ desks

Write the number shown by the quick picture.

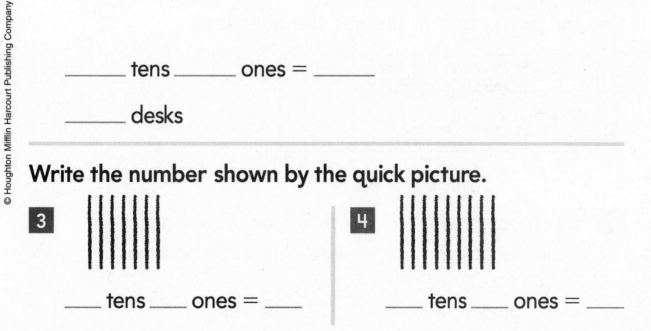

3 _____ tens _____ ones = _____

4 _____ tens _____ ones = _____

Test Prep

Fill in the bubble next to the correct answer.

5 Dev has 5 bags of marbles. There are 10 marbles in each bag. How many marbles does Dev have?

○ 5 marbles ○ 10 marbles ○ 50 marbles

6 Which number is shown by the quick picture?

| | | | | | | |

○ 80 ○ 50 ○ 30

7 Which is the same number as 4 tens 0 ones?

○ 4 ○ 10 ○ 40

Spiral Review

Use the bar graph to answer the questions.

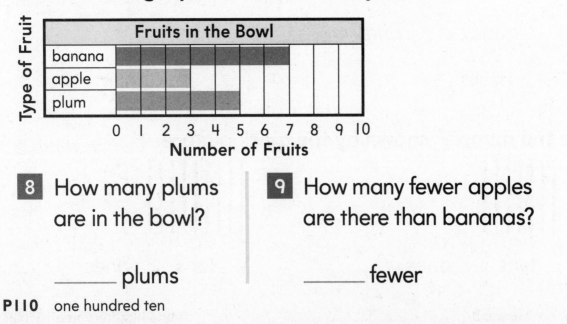

8 How many plums are in the bowl?

_____ plums

9 How many fewer apples are there than bananas?

_____ fewer

Count to 120

1	2	3	4	5	6	7	8	9	10
11	12	13	14	15	16	17	18	19	20
21	22	23	24	25	26	27	28	29	30
31	32	33	34	35	36	37	38	39	40
41	42	43	44	45	46	47	48	49	50
51	52	53	54	55	56	57	58	59	60
61	62	63	64	65	66	67	68	69	70
71	72	73	74	75	76	77	78	79	80
81	82	83	84	85	86	87	88	89	90
91	92	93	94	95	96	97	98	99	100
101	102	103	104	105	106	107	108	109	110
111	112	113	114	115	116	117	118	119	120

**Use the counting chart. Count by ones.
Write the next 5 numbers.**

1 114, _____, _____, _____, _____, _____

2 97, _____, _____, _____, _____, _____

3 21, _____, _____, _____, _____, _____

4 24 stamps are inside a book.
6 stamps are outside the book.
Count by ones to find
the total number of stamps.

24 | _____, _____, _____, _____, _____, _____

_____ stamps

Test Prep

Fill in the bubble next to the correct answer.

5 Use the counting chart
to count by ones.
Which numbers come next?

1	2	3	4	5	6	7	8	9	10
11	12	13	14	15	16	17	18	19	20
21	22	23	24	25	26	27	28	29	30
31	32	33	34	35	36	37	38	39	40
41	42	43	44	45	46	47	48	49	50
51	52	53	54	55	56	57	58	59	60
61	62	63	64	65	66	67	68	69	70
71	72	73	74	75	76	77	78	79	80
81	82	83	84	85	86	87	88	89	90
91	92	93	94	95	96	97	98	99	100
101	102	103	104	105	106	107	108	109	110
111	112	113	114	115	116	117	118	119	120

99,

- ○ 100, 101, 102
- ○ 100, 110, 120
- ○ 98, 97, 96

6 There are 20 coins inside a jar
and 5 coins outside the jar.
How many coins are there in all?
Count to solve.

- ○ 21 coins   ○ 24 coins   ○ 25 coins

Spiral Review

**Write the sum. Change the order
of the addends and add again.**

7 8 + 7 = _____   _____ + _____ = _____

8 _____ = 9 + 4   _____ = _____ + _____

LESSON 10.2
**More Practice/
Homework**

ONLINE
Video Tutorials and
Interactive Examples

Represent Numbers as Tens and Ones with Objects

1 **Math on the Spot**

I am a number less than 40.
I have 5 ones and some tens.
What number could I be?

_____

2 (MP) **Use Tools** Ricky uses tens and ones to show the number of cans on a shelf. How many cans are there?

_____ tens _____ ones = _____

There are _____ cans on the shelf.

Write the number.

3

_____ tens _____ ones = _____

Test Prep

Fill in the bubble next to the correct answer.

4 Roger has 56 .
How many tens and ones can he make?

○ 5 tens 6 ones

○ 6 tens 5 ones

○ 5 tens 9 ones

5 Which number does the picture show?

○ 13   ○ 36   ○ 63

6 Which shows the number 26?

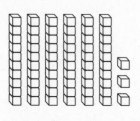

Spiral Review

**Solve. Then circle the pair of facts
if they are related.**

7 $14 - 8 =$ _____

$6 + 8 =$ _____

8 $16 - 7 =$ _____

$7 + 8 =$ _____

LESSON 10.3
**More Practice/
Homework**

 **ONLINE**
Video Tutorials and
Interactive Examples

Represent Numbers as Tens and Ones with Drawings

1 Melanie has 73 feathers. Draw a quick picture to show the number of feathers. Write how many tens and ones.

Tens	Ones

73 = _____ tens _____ ones

2 Tommy has 96 rocks. Draw a quick picture to show the number of rocks Tommy has. Write how many tens and ones.

Tens	Ones

96 = _____ tens _____ ones

3 (MP) **Use Structure** Bernard draws this picture to show the coins in his collection. What number does his picture show? Write the number as tens and ones.

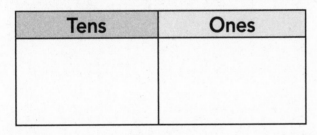

_____ = _____ tens _____ ones

Test Prep

Fill in the bubble next to the correct answer.

4 Sarah has 56 ⬡. Which quick picture shows how many tens and ones she can make?

○   ○   ○

___

5 Which number does the quick picture show?

○ 37   ○ 70   ○ 72

___

6 Which number does the quick picture show?

○ 22   ○ 17   ○ 12

Spiral Review

Use subtraction to find the unknown addend.

7 Solve 5 + ⬛ = 14.

_____ − _____ = _____

5 + _____ = 14

Name _____

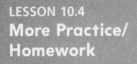
Decompose Numbers in Different Ways

1 **Open Ended** Write a two-digit number.
Draw two different ways to show your number.

My Number: _____

Tens	Ones

Tens	Ones

2 Draw quick pictures to show
the number 86 in two different ways.

Tens	Ones

Tens	Ones

3 **(MP)** **Use Structure** Circle each picture
that shows the number 37.

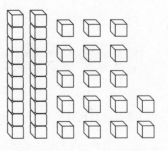

Test Prep

Fill in the bubble next to the correct answer.

4 Marcie shows the number 62 in different ways. Which is not a way to show 62?

○ |||||| °°
       °°
       °°
       °°°
       °°°

○ || °
     °
     °
     °
     °°

○ ||||||| °
           °

---

5 One way to show 25 is 25 ones. Which is a different way to show 25?

○ | °°°
    °°°
    °°°
    °°°
    °°°

○ | °°
    °°
    °°
    °°
    °°

○ | °°°°
    °°°°
    °°°°
    °°°°
    °°°°

---

6 What number does the picture show? Write the number.

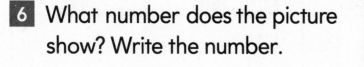

_____

Spiral Review

7 How many more ● are there than ●?

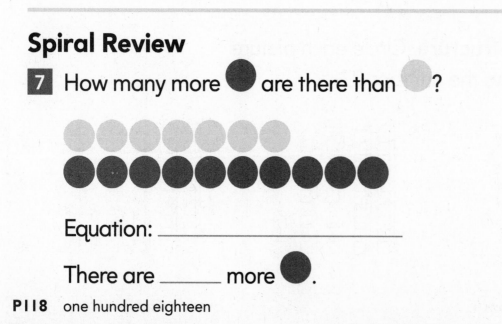

Equation: _____

There are _____ more ●.

Name _____

LESSON 10.5
**More Practice/
Homework**

🍎 Ed **ONLINE**
Video Tutorials and
Interactive Examples

Represent, Read, and Write Numbers from 100 to 110

1 MP **Use Structure** Each seat has a number.
Shirley says her seat number is
the same as 10 tens and 6 more ones.
What is the seat number?
Draw a quick picture to show the number.

Seat number _____

Write the number.

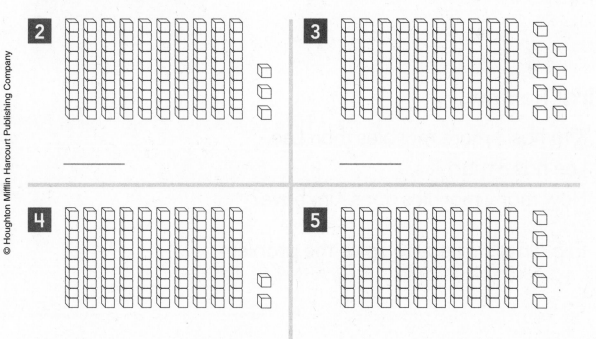

Test Prep

Fill in the bubble next to the correct answer.

6 Which number does the picture show?

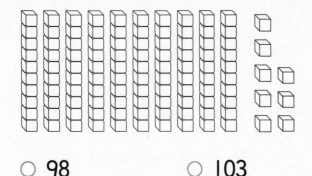

- ○ 98
- ○ 103
- ○ 108

Write the number.

7

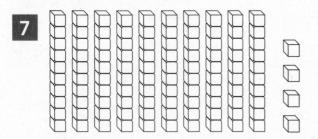

_____

Spiral Review

8 Kim has 3 more marbles than Lee.
Lee has 8 marbles.
How many marbles does Kim have?

Explain a strategy to solve the problem.

_____

_____

LESSON 10.6
**More Practice/
Homework**

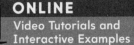
ONLINE
Video Tutorials and
Interactive Examples

Represent, Read, and Write Numbers from 110 to 120

1 (MP) **Use Structure** Amber counts her stickers. She makes 11 groups of 10 stickers each, with 7 extra stickers. How many stickers does she have? Draw to show your thinking.

_____ stickers

Write the number.

2

_____

3

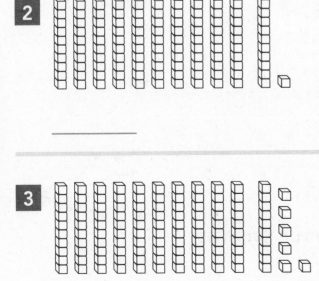

_____

one hundred twenty-one **P121**

Test Prep

Fill in the bubble next to the correct answer.

4 Which number does the picture show?

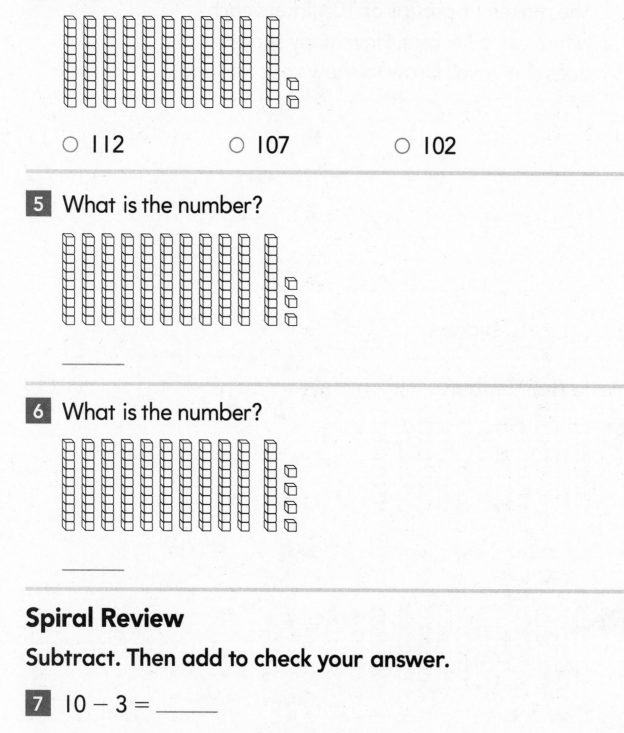

○ 112   ○ 107   ○ 102

5 What is the number?

_____

6 What is the number?

_____

Spiral Review

Subtract. Then add to check your answer.

7 $10 - 3 =$ _____

_____ + _____ = _____

Name _____

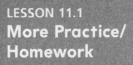
Understand Greater Than

1 (MP) **Reason** Tom has 64 stamps.
Marcia has 43 stamps.
Who has more stamps?

Draw a quick picture to show
the numbers. Then solve.

_____ is greater than _____.

_____ has more stamps.

2 **Math on the Spot** Pam and Jake play a game
for points. Pam's points are 2 ones and 8 tens.
Jake's points are 2 tens and 8 ones.
Who has the greater number of points?

_____

Compare the numbers to find which is greater.

3 Compare 44 and 75.

_____ is greater than _____.

4 Compare 46 and 41.

_____ is greater than _____.

5 Compare 72 and 27.

_____ is greater than _____.

6 Compare 45 and 75.

_____ is greater than _____.

Test Prep

Fill in the bubble next to the correct answer.

7 Ellen and Ty bake muffins. Ellen bakes 36 muffins. Ty bakes a greater number of muffins than Ellen. How many muffins could Ty bake?

○ 26 muffins   ○ 29 muffins   ○ 38 muffins

8 Which number is greater than 75?

○ 82   ○ 70   ○ 65

Spiral Review

Draw ◯. Write an equation.

9 Mel has 6 pens. Amir has 6 more pens than Mel. How many pens does Amir have?

Equation: _____

Amir has _____ pens.

10 Tracy sees 12 birds. Yan sees 4 fewer birds than Tracy. How many birds does Yan see?

Equation: _____

Yan sees _____ birds.

Understand Less Than

1 (MP) **Construct Arguments**
Explain why 45 is less than 54.

_____

_____

2 Karen counts 22 fish in a pond.
Miriam counts 32 fish.
Who counts fewer fish?

_____ counts fewer fish.

3 **Math on the Spot** Jack makes the number 84.
Kit makes a number that has fewer ones
than 84 and fewer tens than 4 tens.
What could be a number Kit makes?

_____

Compare the numbers to find which is less.

4 Compare 88 and 78.

_____ is less than _____.

5 Compare 37 and 52.

_____ is less than _____.

6 Compare 93 and 99.

_____ is less than _____.

7 Compare 63 and 36.

_____ is less than _____.

Test Prep

Fill in the bubble next to the correct answer.

8 Ross and Austin paint rocks.
Ross paints 45 rocks.
Austin paints fewer rocks than Ross.
How many rocks could Austin paint?

○ 54 rocks   ○ 48 rocks   ○ 42 rocks

9 Which number is less than 91?

○ 99   ○ 92   ○ 19

10 Which number is less than 23?

○ 11   ○ 31   ○ 33

Spiral Review

Count forward.
Write the next 5 numbers.

11 25, _____, _____, _____, _____, _____

12 98, _____, _____, _____, _____, _____

13 86, _____, _____, _____, _____, _____

14 110, _____, _____, _____, _____, _____

LESSON 11.3
**More Practice/
Homework**

 ONLINE
Video Tutorials and
Interactive Examples

Use Symbols to Compare

1 **Math on the Spot** Gil won 48 tokens.
Rob won 65 tokens. 50 tokens are needed
for a teddy bear prize. Which friend has
enough tokens for the prize?

_____ has enough tokens for the prize.

2 (MP) **Reason** Angel has 8 pretzels.
Grant has 18 pretzels.
Who has fewer pretzels?
Compare the numbers to solve.

_____ ◯ _____

_____ has fewer pretzels.

Write <, >, or =.

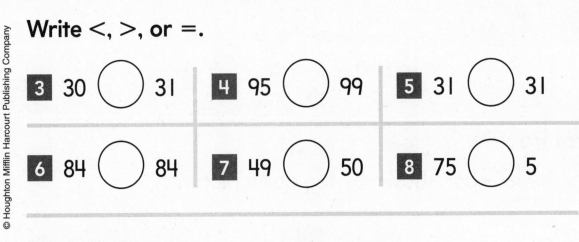

3 30 ◯ 31   **4** 95 ◯ 99   **5** 31 ◯ 31

6 84 ◯ 84   **7** 49 ◯ 50   **8** 75 ◯ 5

Open Ended Write a number to make
the comparison true.

9 _____ > 83   _____ < 83   _____ = 83

Test Prep

Write <, >, or =.

10 61 ◯ 59	**11** 26 ◯ 32	**12** 15 ◯ 9
13 72 ◯ 72	**14** 48 ◯ 39	**15** 53 ◯ 58

Fill in the bubble next to the correct answer.

16 Which number makes the comparison true?

25 < ▮

○ 21   ○ 25   ○ 28

17 Which number makes the comparison true?

▮ > 39

○ 9   ○ 30   ○ 41

Spiral Review

Write the number shown by the quick picture.

18 _____

19 _____

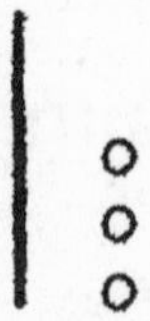

LESSON 11.4
**More Practice/
Homework**

ONLINE
Video Tutorials and
Interactive Examples

Compare Numbers

(MP) **Use Repeated Reasoning**
Compare numbers to solve.

1 Phil and his friends collect baseball cards.
Phil has 32 cards. Eric has 48 cards.
Lonnie has more cards than Phil
but fewer cards than Eric.
How many cards does Lonnie have?

Number of Baseball Cards				
32	84	44	51	48

Lonnie has _____ baseball cards.

2 My number is greater than 40
and less than 45. Which of these
could be my number?
Circle the number.

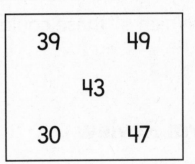

39   49
        43
30   47

3 **Open Ended** Write a number to solve.

Write a number less than 52. _____

Write a number greater than 52. _____

Write <, >, or =.

4 28 ◯ 20   **5** 85 ◯ 99   **6** 75 ◯ 75

Test Prep

Fill in the bubble next to the correct answer.

7 Carlos has 60 rocks in his collection.
Sam has 58 rocks. Kai has fewer rocks
than Carlos but more than Sam.
How many rocks does Kai have?

○ 57 rocks   ○ 59 rocks   ○ 61 rocks

8 My number is greater than 28 and less than 35.
Which of these could be my number?

○ 25   ○ 32   ○ 38

9 My number is less than 81 and greater than 74.
Which of these could be my number?

○ 18   ○ 71   ○ 76

Spiral Review

Solve. Draw to show your work.

10 Some children play in the park.
Then 6 more children come to play.
Now there are 13 children.
How many children were playing to start?

Equation: _____

_____ children

© Houghton Mifflin Harcourt Publishing Company

Name _____

LESSON 12.1
**More Practice/
Homework**

ONLINE
Video Tutorials and
Interactive Examples

Represent Adding Tens

(MP) **Model with Mathematics** Draw tens to
show the problem. Write an equation to solve.

1 Tommy sees 30 carrots. Earl sees
20 carrots. How many carrots do
Tommy and Earl see?

Equation: _____

They see _____ carrots.

2 Bill plants 10 seeds in a garden.
Then he plants 60 more seeds.
How many seeds does Bill plant?

Equation: _____

Bill plants _____ seeds.

3 30 ants are on a log. Then 60
more join them. How many ants
are on the log now?

Equation: _____

_____ ants are on the log.

Test Prep

Fill in the bubble next to the correct answer.

4 Which shows how to add 40 + 30?

○ 4 ones + 3 ones = 7 ones

○ 4 tens + 3 tens = 7 tens

○ 40 tens + 30 tens = 70 tens

5 A farmer sells 50 white eggs and 20 brown eggs. How many eggs does the farmer sell?

○ 30 eggs

○ 40 eggs

○ 70 eggs

Spiral Review

Draw to show your work. Solve.

6 Gina has some flowers. She gives 7 flowers to friends. Now she has 6 flowers. How many flowers does Gina have to start?

_____ flowers

LESSON 12.2
**More Practice/
Homework**

ONLINE
Video Tutorials and
Interactive Examples

Represent Subtracting Tens

Draw tens to show your work. Solve.

1 **Reason** There are 50 crabs on the beach. 30 crabs walk away. How many crabs are on the beach now?

Equation: _____

_____ crabs

2 **Math on the Spot** Jeff has 40 pennies. He gives some to Jill. He has 10 pennies left. How many pennies does Jeff give to Jill?

Equation: _____

_____ pennies

3 $60 - 30 =$ _____

6 tens $-$ 3 tens $=$ _____ tens

4 _____ $= 80 - 20$

_____ tens $=$ 8 tens $-$ 2 tens

Test Prep

Fill in the bubble next to the correct answer.

5 Meg has a box of 50 crayons. She takes out 20 crayons. How many crayons are still in the box?

○ 30 crayons

○ 40 crayons

○ 70 crayons

6 Which shows how to subtract 70 – 10?

○ 70 tens – 10 tens = 60 tens

○ 7 ones – 1 one = 6 ones

○ 7 tens – 1 ten = 6 tens

Spiral Review

Write the number shown by the quick picture.

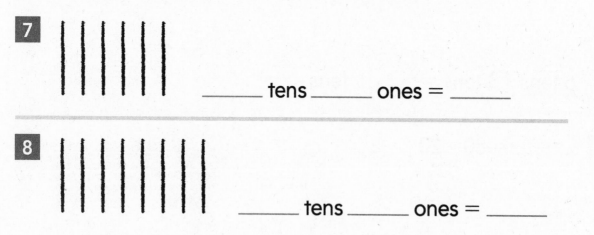

7 _____ tens _____ ones = _____

8 _____ tens _____ ones = _____

Add or Subtract Tens

(MP) **Model with Mathematics** Write an addition or subtraction equation to solve.

Greetings from Florida!

1 Cindy has 30 postcards. Then she finds 10 more postcards. How many postcards does Cindy have now?

Equation: _____

_____ postcards

2 There are 40 dogs at the dog park. Then 20 dogs go home. How many dogs are at the dog park now?

Equation: _____

_____ dogs

3 Lila and Stan count 50 oranges. Lila counts 30 oranges. How many oranges does Stan count?

Equation: _____

_____ oranges

Add or subtract.

4 $60 + \_\_\_\_ = 90$ | **5** $\_\_\_\_ = 50 + 30$ | **6** $70 - 20 = \_\_\_\_$

Test Prep

Fill in the bubble next to the correct answer.

7 Mr. Jones catches 30 fish.
Mr. Smith catches 50 fish.
How many fish do they catch?

○ 20 fish

○ 60 fish

○ 80 fish

8 A store has 60 books. They sell 20 books.
How many books does the store have now?

○ 30 books

○ 40 books

○ 80 books

Solve.

9 $90 - 20 = $ _____   **10** _____ $ + 20 = 40$

Spiral Review

Count back to subtract.

11 $10 - 1 = $ _____   **12** $7 - 3 = $ _____

13 $8 - 2 = $ _____   **14** $9 - 2 = $ _____

Name _____

LESSON 12.4
More Practice/ Homework

ONLINE
Video Tutorials and
Interactive Examples

Use a Hundred Chart to Add

Use the hundred chart to solve.

1 (MP) **Use Tools** Arthur has 11 books. Kristen gives him 5 more books. How many books does Arthur have now? Write the equation.

1	2	3	4	5	6	7	8	9	10
11	12	13	14	15	16	17	18	19	20
21	22	23	24	25	26	27	28	29	30
31	32	33	34	35	36	37	38	39	40
41	42	43	44	45	46	47	48	49	50
51	52	53	54	55	56	57	58	59	60
61	62	63	64	65	66	67	68	69	70
71	72	73	74	75	76	77	78	79	80
81	82	83	84	85	86	87	88	89	90
91	92	93	94	95	96	97	98	99	100

Equation: _____

_____ books

2 Crabs come in different sizes and colors. There are 37 red crabs and 5 purple crabs on the beach. How many crabs are on the beach? Write the equation.

Equation: _____

_____ crabs

3 (MP) **Model with Mathematics** There are 25 books on the shelf. Tia puts 20 more books on the shelf. How many books are on the shelf now? Write the equation.

Equation: _____ _____ books

Test Prep

Use the hundred chart to solve. Fill in the bubble next to the correct answer.

4 A store sells 25 blue shirts and 10 yellow shirts. How many shirts does the store sell?

1	2	3	4	5	6	7	8	9	10
11	12	13	14	15	16	17	18	19	20
21	22	23	24	25	26	27	28	29	30
31	32	33	34	35	36	37	38	39	40
41	42	43	44	45	46	47	48	49	50
51	52	53	54	55	56	57	58	59	60
61	62	63	64	65	66	67	68	69	70
71	72	73	74	75	76	77	78	79	80
81	82	83	84	85	86	87	88	89	90
91	92	93	94	95	96	97	98	99	100

○ 26 shirts

○ 34 shirts

○ 35 shirts

5 There are 68 bugs in the grass. Then 3 more come. How many bugs are in the grass now?

○ 70 bugs   ○ 71 bugs   ○ 98 bugs

Spiral Review

Write an equation to solve. Draw to show your thinking.

6 Jen has 12 grapes. She gives 5 to Keith. How many grapes does Jen have now?

Equation: _____

_____ grapes

Name _____

LESSON 12.5
More Practice/ Homework

 **ONLINE**
Video Tutorials and
Interactive Examples

Represent Addition with Tens and Ones

(MP) Model with Mathematics Use tens and ones to add. Show your work.

1 Kim has 25 toy dogs. She gets 2 more toy dogs. How many toy dogs does Kim have now?

Equation: _____

_____ toy dogs

2 Ben sees 34 yellow balloons and 4 red balloons. How many balloons does he see?

Equation: _____

_____ balloons

3 Dan has 15 acorns. He finds 20 more acorns. How many acorns does Dan have now?

Equation: _____

_____ acorns

Solve the equations.

4 $8 + 31 =$ _____   **5** $60 + 3 =$ _____

6 _____ $= 80 + 5$ **7** _____ $= 30 + 15$

Test Prep

Fill in the bubble next to the correct answer.

8 Jack sees 26 apple trees and 3 peach trees. How many trees does he see?

○ 23 trees

○ 29 trees

○ 56 trees

Solve the equations.

9 _____ = 50 + 2

10 24 + 5 = _____

11 12 + 7 = _____

12 34 + 40 = _____

13 82 + 6 = _____

14 _____ = 20 + 43

Spiral Review

15 Circle each picture that shows 44.

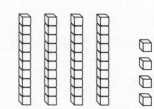

© Houghton Mifflin Harcourt Publishing Company

Represent Make Ten to Add

(MP) **Use Structure** Make a ten to solve.
Show your work.

1 Mark has 63 shells. Then he finds 8 more.
How many shells does he have now?

Equation: _____

_____ shells

2 There are 59 red tomatoes and 5 green
tomatoes. How many tomatoes are there?

Equation: _____

_____ tomatoes

3 Kayla has 8 peaches and 53 pears. How
many peaches and pears does she have?

Equation: _____

_____ peaches and pears

Make a ten to solve.

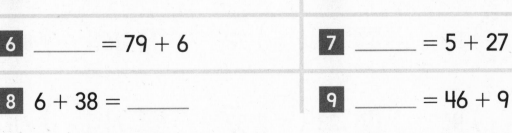

4 $8 + 45 =$ _____

5 $27 + 4 =$ _____

6 _____ $= 79 + 6$

7 _____ $= 5 + 27$

8 $6 + 38 =$ _____

9 _____ $= 46 + 9$

Test Prep

Make a ten to solve. Fill in the bubble next to the correct answer.

10 Cora has 36 buttons. She finds 6 more. How many buttons does she have now?

○ 30 buttons

○ 32 buttons

○ 42 buttons

11 Hank puts 18 red roses and 6 white roses in a vase. How many roses are in the vase?

○ 28 roses

○ 24 roses

○ 12 roses

Make a ten to solve.

12 56 + 8 = _____

13 78 + 7 = _____

14 _____ = 68 + 5

Spiral Review

Write <, >, or =.

15 94 ◯ 85

16 64 ◯ 72

17 36 ◯ 83

18 45 ◯ 45

19 23 ◯ 32

20 71 ◯ 71

Represent Make Ten to Add with a Visual Model

Make a ten to solve. Write the numbers.

1 (MP) **Model with Mathematics** There are 26 children in a race. Then 6 more children join them. How many children are in the race now?

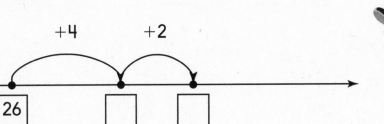

+4   +2

[26]   [ ]   [ ]

Equation: _____

_____ children

---

2 (MP) **Attend to Precision** There are 19 swimmers in a pool. 6 more swimmers get in the pool. How many swimmers are there now?

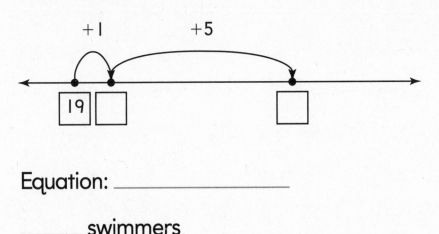

+1   +5

[19][ ]   [ ]

Equation: _____

_____ swimmers

Test Prep

Fill in the bubble next to the correct answer.

3 Which number line shows how to make a ten to add 16 + 6?

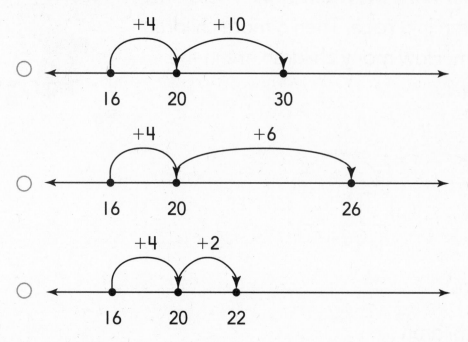

○ +4   +10

16   20   30

○ +4   +6

16   20   26

○ +4   +2

16   20   22

Spiral Review

Write the number.

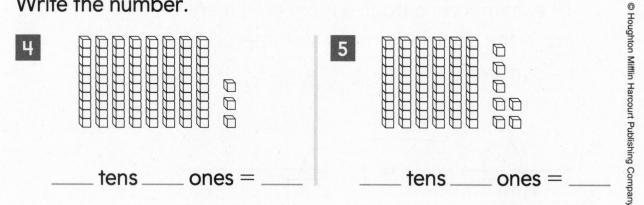

4 _____ tens _____ ones = _____

5 _____ tens _____ ones = _____

LESSON 12.8
**More Practice/
Homework**

ONLINE
Video Tutorials and
Interactive Examples

Use Mental Math to Find 10 Less and 10 More

1 **(MP) Reason** Julius, Terry, and Heather each have a stamp collection. Julius has 75 stamps. Terry has 10 fewer stamps than Julius. Heather has 10 fewer stamps than Terry. How many stamps do Terry and Heather each have?

A. Write the number of stamps Terry and Heather each have.

Terry has _____ stamps.   Heather has _____ stamps.

B. How many more stamps does Terry have than Heather? Explain your reasoning.

_____

_____

2 **Math on the Spot** I have 76 rocks. I want to collect 10 more. How many rocks will I have then?

_____ rocks

Write the numbers that are 10 less and 10 more.

| 3 | _____ 32 _____ | 4 | _____ 70 _____ |
| 5 | _____ 68 _____ | 6 | _____ 44 _____ |

Test Prep

Fill in the bubble next to the correct answer.

7 Which number is 10 more than 47?

○ 37   ○ 48   ○ 57

8 Which number is 10 less than 81?

○ 71   ○ 80   ○ 91

9 Alex has 54 books. Jane has 10 more books than Alex. How many books does Jane have?

○ 44 books   ○ 55 books   ○ 64 books

Spiral Review

Solve. Draw or write to show your thinking.

10 Karen has 6 teddy bears. Mandy has 3 teddy bears. Kirsten has 4 teddy bears. How many teddy bears do they have in all?

_____ teddy bears

Solve each equation.

11 _____ = 41 + 5

12 60 + 8 = _____

13 _____ = 36 + 3

14 4 + 72 = _____

© Houghton Mifflin Harcourt Publishing Company

LESSON 13.1
**More Practice/
Homework**

 ONLINE
Video Tutorials and
Interactive Examples

Use a Hundred Chart to Show Two-Digit Addition and Subtraction

(MP) **Reason** Use the hundred chart to solve.

1 There are 43 cherries in a bowl. Some more cherries are put in the bowl. Now there are 63 cherries in the bowl. How many cherries are put in the bowl?

_____ cherries

1	2	3	4	5	6	7	8	9	10
11	12	13	14	15	16	17	18	19	20
21	22	23	24	25	26	27	28	29	30
31	32	33	34	35	36	37	38	39	40
41	42	43	44	45	46	47	48	49	50
51	52	53	54	55	56	57	58	59	60
61	62	63	64	65	66	67	68	69	70
71	72	73	74	75	76	77	78	79	80
81	82	83	84	85	86	87	88	89	90
91	92	93	94	95	96	97	98	99	100

2 Markus has 40 pennies. He gives some to Jill. He has 10 pennies left. How many pennies does Markus give to Jill?

_____ pennies

3 Alison sees 22 roses. Monte sees some roses. Alison and Monte see 52 roses together. How many roses does Monte see?

_____ roses

4 $80 - 20 =$ _____

5 $70 - 50 =$ _____

6 $26 + 30 =$ _____

7 $49 + 50 =$ _____

Test Prep

Fill in the bubble next to the correct answer.

1	2	3	4	5	6	7	8	9	10
11	12	13	14	15	16	17	18	19	20
21	22	23	24	25	26	27	28	29	30
31	32	33	34	35	36	37	38	39	40
41	42	43	44	45	46	47	48	49	50
51	52	53	54	55	56	57	58	59	60
61	62	63	64	65	66	67	68	69	70
71	72	73	74	75	76	77	78	79	80
81	82	83	84	85	86	87	88	89	90
91	92	93	94	95	96	97	98	99	100

8 There are 17 ants on a branch. Some more ants come. Now there are 37 ants on the branch. How many ants come?

○ 17 ants   ○ 20 ants   ○ 30 ants

9 A tank has 30 fish in it. Some fish are taken out. Now there are 20 fish in the tank. How many fish are taken out?

○ 40 fish   ○ 20 fish   ○ 10 fish

Spiral Review

10 Write the number.

_____

11 Write the number three different ways.

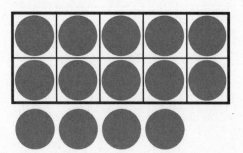

_____ + _____

_____ ten _____ ones

_____

LESSON 13.2
**More Practice/
Homework**

ONLINE
Video Tutorials and
Interactive Examples

Understand and Explain Place Value Addition

Draw to show the numbers. Use tens and ones to add.

1 (MP) **Attend to Precision** There are 34 ducks in a pond. 12 more ducks join them. How many ducks are in the pond now?

Tens	Ones

3 tens   4 ones   34
+ 1 ten   + 2 ones   + 12
_____ tens + _____ ones

_____ + _____ = _____

---

2 Solve 54 + 33.

Tens	Ones

5 tens   4 ones   54
+ 3 tens   + 3 ones   + 33
_____ tens + _____ ones

_____ + _____ = _____

---

3 Solve 29 + 58.

Tens	Ones

2 tens   9 ones   29
+ 5 tens   + 8 ones   + 58
_____ tens + _____ ones

_____ + _____ = _____

Test Prep

Fill in the bubble next to the correct answer.

4 Alex counts 23 beans. Marta counts 43 beans.
How many beans do they count in all?

○ 27 beans   ○ 55 beans   ○ 66 beans

5 Kelli sees 15 lemons and 26 limes.
How many lemons and limes does Kelli see?

○ 31   ○ 41   ○ 47

Spiral Review

Use the hundred chart to solve.

6 Greg has 38 marbles. He gets 20 more marbles. How many marbles does Greg have?

Equation: _____

_____ marbles

1	2	3	4	5	6	7	8	9	10
11	12	13	14	15	16	17	18	19	20
21	22	23	24	25	26	27	28	29	30
31	32	33	34	35	36	37	38	39	40
41	42	43	44	45	46	47	48	49	50
51	52	53	54	55	56	57	58	59	60
61	62	63	64	65	66	67	68	69	70
71	72	73	74	75	76	77	78	79	80
81	82	83	84	85	86	87	88	89	90
91	92	93	94	95	96	97	98	99	100

Compare the numbers to find which is less.

7 Compare 36 and 63.

_____ is less than _____.

8 Compare 86 and 68.

_____ is less than _____.

Understand and Explain Place Value Subtraction

Use tens to subtract.

1 (MP) **Reason** Nikki collects 80 shells. She gives 50 shells to her brother. How many shells does she have now?

_____ shells

Tens	Ones

8	tens		0	ones
−5	tens	−	0	ones
___	tens		___	ones

80
−50
_____

2 (MP) **Reason** Chris has 50 buttons. He gives Jenna 10 buttons. How many buttons does Chris still have?

_____ buttons

Tens	Ones

5	tens		0	ones
−1	tens	−	0	ones
___	tens		___	ones

50
−10
_____

3

70
−20
____

Tens	Ones

7	tens		0	ones
−2	tens	−	0	ones
___	tens		___	ones

Test Prep

Fill in the bubble next to the correct answer.

4 There are 60 children at the playground. 40 children leave the playground. How many children are still on the playground?

   ○ 10 children   ○ 20 children   ○ 30 children

5 There are 80 pears in a basket. 20 pears are sold. How many pears are in the basket now?

   ○ 60 pears   ○ 40 pears   ○ 30 pears

Spiral Review

Complete the bar model. Write an equation.

6 Ehrin has 9 pencils. Jeff has 3 fewer pencils than Ehrin. How many pencils does Jeff have?

Equation: _____

Jeff has _____ pencils.

7 Ben has 7 balloons. He gets some more. Now he has 16 balloons. How many balloons does he get?

Equation: _____

_____ balloons

Name _____

LESSON 13.4
More Practice/ Homework

ONLINE
Video Tutorials and
Interactive Examples

Solve Two-Digit Addition and Subtraction Problems

(MP) **Reason** Solve.

1 Ellie plants 80 seeds.
Leo plants 50 seeds. How
many more seeds does
Ellie plant than Leo?

_____ more seeds

2 Dylan plants 56 seeds. Then he plants
30 more seeds. How many seeds
does he plant?

_____ seeds

3 Simone plants 48 bean seeds and
27 pea seeds. How many seeds
does she plant in all?

_____ seeds

4 Antonio plants 62 corn seeds and
24 tomato seeds. How many seeds
does he plant?

_____ seeds

Test Prep

Fill in the bubble next to the correct answer.

5 Ms. Duncan has 50 tomatoes. She gives
some to Kelly. Now she has 40 tomatoes.
How many tomatoes does she give Kelly?

    ○ 40 tomatoes   ○ 30 tomatoes   ○ 10 tomatoes

6 There are 33 rows of yellow corn and 45 rows
of white corn in a field. How many rows of
corn are in the field?

    ○ 73 rows   ○ 78 rows   ○ 80 rows

Spiral Review

7 Mason gives away number cards that are
less than 24 or more than 33. Circle the
number card he could give away.

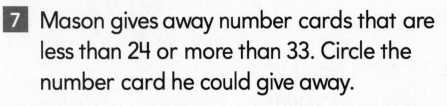

| 28 | 25 | 22 | 32 |

Write <, >, or =.

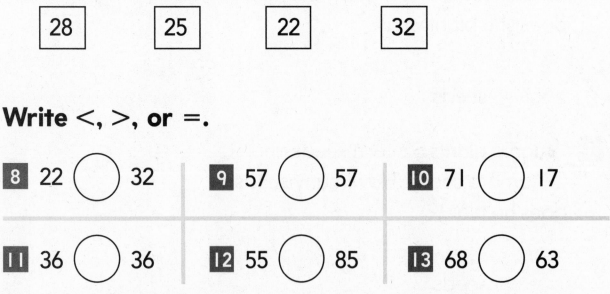

8 22 ◯ 32   **9** 57 ◯ 57   **10** 71 ◯ 17

11 36 ◯ 36   **12** 55 ◯ 85   **13** 68 ◯ 63

LESSON 13.5
**More Practice/
Homework**

Ed **ONLINE**
Video Tutorials and
Interactive Examples

Practice Facts to 20

Add or subtract to solve.

1 Jake has 7 baseball bats. Caroline has
6 softball bats. How many bats do they have?

_____ bats

2 **Open Ended** Ave sees 12 pink and white
flowers. How many flowers could be pink and
how many flowers could be white?

_____ white flowers   _____ pink flower

3 **Math on the Spot** Jamal thinks of an addition
fact. The sum is 15. One addend is 8. What is a
fact Jamal could be thinking of?

____ ◯ ____ ◯ ____

4 $2 + 4 = $ _____

5 _____ $= 10 + 2$

6 _____ $= 15 - 9$

7 $14 - 8 = $ _____

8 6
  $+ 3$

9 8
  $+ 4$

10 13
   $- 5$

11 7
   $- 7$

12 7
   $+ 5$

13 18
   $- 9$

14 6
   $- 3$

15 9
   $+ 7$

Test Prep

Fill in the bubble next to the correct answer.

16 Kathy has 11 oranges. She gives 3 oranges to Jamal. How many oranges does Kathy have now?

○ 8 oranges   ○ 9 oranges   ○ 10 oranges

17 Which fact has a sum of 9?

○ 4 + 3   ○ 3 + 6   ○ 6 + 4

18 Which fact has a sum of 13?

○ 7 + 5   ○ 8 + 6   ○ 7 + 6

Spiral Review

Make a ten to solve. Write the numbers.

19 Mrs. Shaw has 37 paint jars. She gets 7 more paint jars. How many paint jars does she have now?

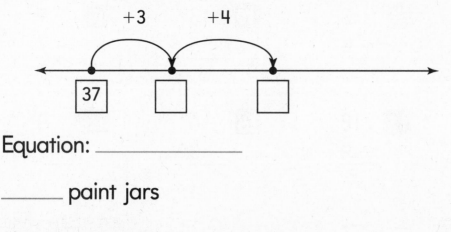

Equation: _____

_____ paint jars

LESSON 13.6
**More Practice/
Homework**

ONLINE
Video Tutorials and
Interactive Examples

Practice Two-Digit Addition and Subtraction

(MP) **Reason** Add or subtract to solve.

1 Owen bikes 15 miles before lunch and 23 miles after lunch. How many miles does Owen bike?

_____ miles

2 Drake has 70 marbles. He gives 40 marbles to Pat. How many marbles does Drake have now?

_____ marbles

3 Tracy draws 36 stars. Then she draws 47 more stars. How many stars does Tracy draw?

_____ stars

Solve.

4 _____ = 16 + 50

5 52 + 26 = _____

6
  39
$+ 5$

7
  60
$- 20$

8
  90
$- 10$

9
  34
$+ 47$

Test Prep

Fill in the bubble next to the correct answer.

10 Solve. $34 + 23 = $ ▮

    ○ 36   ○ 57   ○ 64

11 Solve. ▮ $ = 80 - 20$

    ○ 60   ○ 50   ○ 40

Spiral Review

Add or Subtract.

12 $40 + 20 = $ _____   **13** $60 + 10 = $ _____

14 $50 - 30 = $ _____   **15** $90 - 80 = $ _____

16 $27 + 5 = $ _____   **17** $78 + 4 = $ _____

18 Sally has 58 buttons. Draw a quick picture to show the number of buttons she has. Write how many tens and ones.

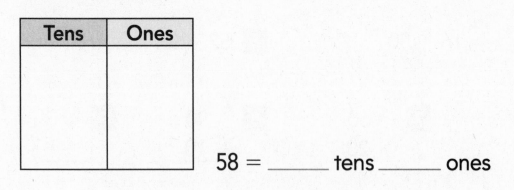

Tens	Ones

$58 = $ _____ tens _____ ones

LESSON 14.1
**More Practice/
Homework**

⊙Ed **ONLINE**
Video Tutorials and
Interactive Examples

Describe and Draw
Three-Dimensional Shapes

cone	cube	cylinder	sphere	rectangular prism

1 ⓂⓅ **Attend to Precision** Trace
the shape that has only 1 flat
surface and a curved surface.
Name the shape.

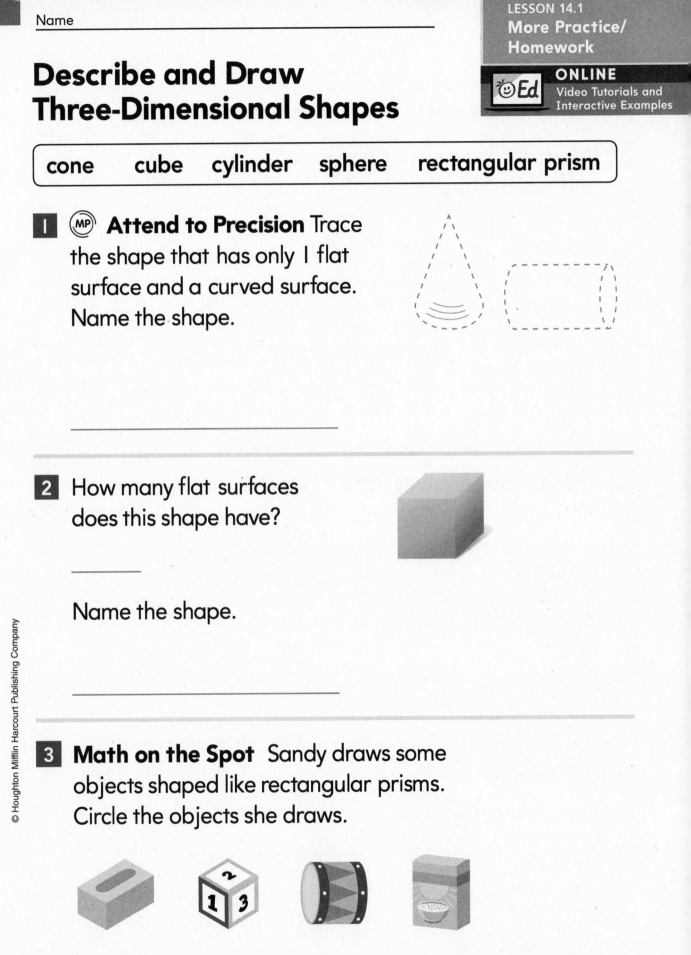

_____

2 How many flat surfaces
does this shape have?

_____

Name the shape.

_____

3 **Math on the Spot** Sandy draws some
objects shaped like rectangular prisms.
Circle the objects she draws.

Test Prep

Fill in the bubble next to the correct answer.

4 Which shape has 2 flat surfaces
and a curved surface?

○

○

○

5 Which shape has only flat surfaces?

○

○

○

Spiral Review

Add or subtract to solve.

6 20 + 19 = _____

7 90 − 40 = _____

8 60 − 40 = _____

9 49 + 5 = _____

LESSON 14.2
**More Practice/
Homework**

ONLINE
Video Tutorials and
Interactive Examples

Compose Three-Dimensional Shapes

1 **Math on the Spot** Circle the ways that make the same shape.

2 (MP) **Use Repeated Reasoning**
Megan stacks the cans.
Circle the name of a combined
shape that she can make.

sphere   cone   cylinder

3 (MP) **Use Structure** How can Ed combine
different shapes to make this shape?

_____

_____

_____

_____

Test Prep

Fill in the bubble next to the correct answer.

4 Liam combines 6 cubes
to make 1 rectangular prism.
Which shape does he make?

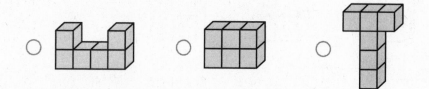

○   ○   ○

5 Which shapes can you combine
to make a large cylinder?

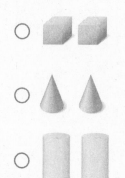

Spiral Review

6 Circle the shape that has only
a curved surface.

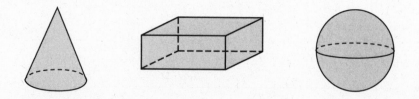

Make New Three-Dimensional Shapes

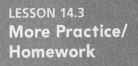

ONLINE
Video Tutorials and Interactive Examples

1 **Math on the Spot** Look at the shape.

How many 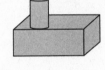 are used to make the shape?

_____ make the shape.

How many are used to make the shape?

_____ make the shape.

---

2 (MP) **Use Repeated Reasoning** Carla makes the shape on the right again and combines both shapes. Circle the new shape.

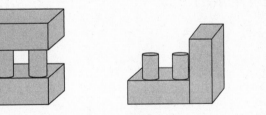 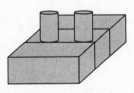

---

3 Max uses two of the same combined shape to make the shape on the right. Circle the combined shape he uses.

Test Prep

Fill in the bubble next to the correct answer.

4 Damien makes this shape.
He makes the shape again.
Then he combines the shapes.
Which new shape can he make?

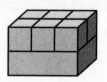

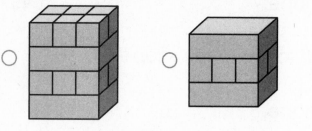

○   ○   ○

5 Lila combines 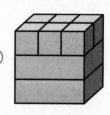, and .

She makes the same shape again
and combines both shapes.
Which new shape can she make?

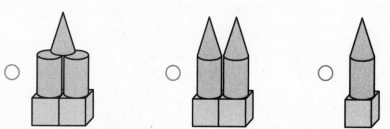

○   ○   ○

Spiral Review

6 Amy makes the shape on the right.
Circle all the shapes she uses.

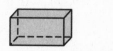

Sort Two-Dimensional Shapes by Attribute

1 Math on the Spot Draw 2 different two-dimensional shapes that follow both parts of the sorting rule.

• 4 sides and 4 vertices

2 ᴹᴾ Use Structure Circle all the ways that describe a square.

• has sides of equal length

• has curved sides

• has 4 straight sides

• has only 3 vertices

3 Open Ended The shapes are sorted into one group. Write to describe how the shapes are sorted.

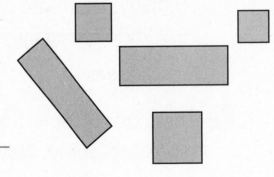

_____

_____

_____

Test Prep

Fill in the bubble next to the correct answer.

4 Which shape has only 3 vertices and 3 straight sides?

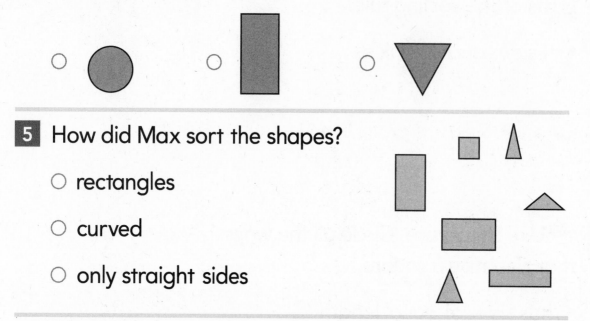

○   ○   ○

5 How did Max sort the shapes?

○ rectangles

○ curved

○ only straight sides

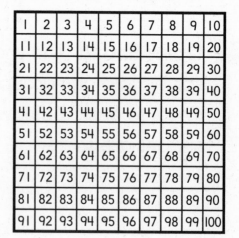

Spiral Review

Use the hundred chart to solve.

6 There are 50 bees. Some bees fly away. There are 30 bees left. How many bees fly away?

_____ bees

7 There are 60 ants. Some more ants come. Now there are 90 ants. How many ants come?

_____ ants

1	2	3	4	5	6	7	8	9	10
11	12	13	14	15	16	17	18	19	20
21	22	23	24	25	26	27	28	29	30
31	32	33	34	35	36	37	38	39	40
41	42	43	44	45	46	47	48	49	50
51	52	53	54	55	56	57	58	59	60
61	62	63	64	65	66	67	68	69	70
71	72	73	74	75	76	77	78	79	80
81	82	83	84	85	86	87	88	89	90
91	92	93	94	95	96	97	98	99	100

LESSON 15.2
**More Practice/
Homework**

ONLINE
Video Tutorials and
Interactive Examples

Describe and Draw
Two-Dimensional Shapes

1 Math on the Spot Draw a picture to solve.

I am a shape with 6 straight sides and
6 vertices.

2 What is the name of the shape?
Circle your answer.

rectangle   trapezoid   triangle

3 A shape has 3 sides and 3 vertices. What is
the name of the shape? Circle your answer.

rectangle   square   triangle

4 (MP) **Attend to Precision** Marnie uses 4 craft
sticks for the straight sides of a shape. Circle
the shape she can make with all 4 sticks.

5 How many sides and vertices does a
trapezoid have?

_____ sides _____ vertices

Test Prep

Fill in the bubble next to the correct answer.

6 Which is the name of the shape?

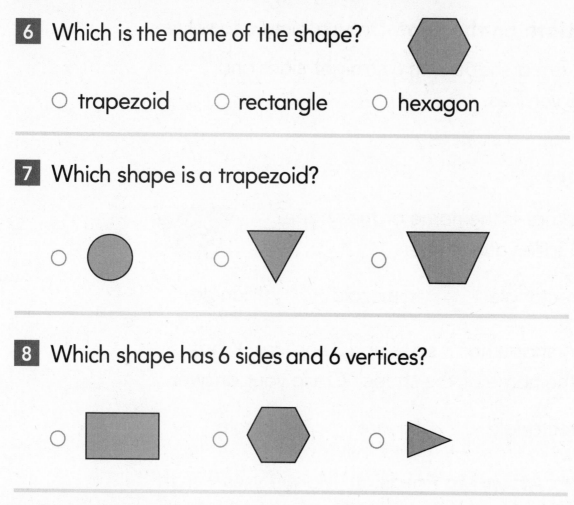

○ trapezoid   ○ rectangle   ○ hexagon

---

7 Which shape is a trapezoid?

○   ○   ○

---

8 Which shape has 6 sides and 6 vertices?

○   ○   ○

Spiral Review

9 Carter builds this shape. He builds the same shape again. Then he puts his combined shapes together. Which new shape can he make?

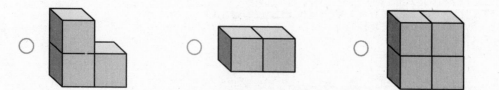

○   ○   ○

Name _____

LESSON 15.3
**More Practice/
Homework**

ONLINE
Video Tutorials and
Interactive Examples

Compose Two-Dimensional Shapes

(MP) **Attend to Precision** Draw to show how to make the new shape.

1 Combine 2 triangles to make a square.

2 Combine 2 trapezoids to make a hexagon.

3 Draw to show how to combine 4 squares to make a large square.

Explain how to put the 4 squares together to make the large square.

_____

_____

Test Prep

Fill in the bubble next to the correct answer.

4 Which shows how to combine 2 rectangles to make a square?

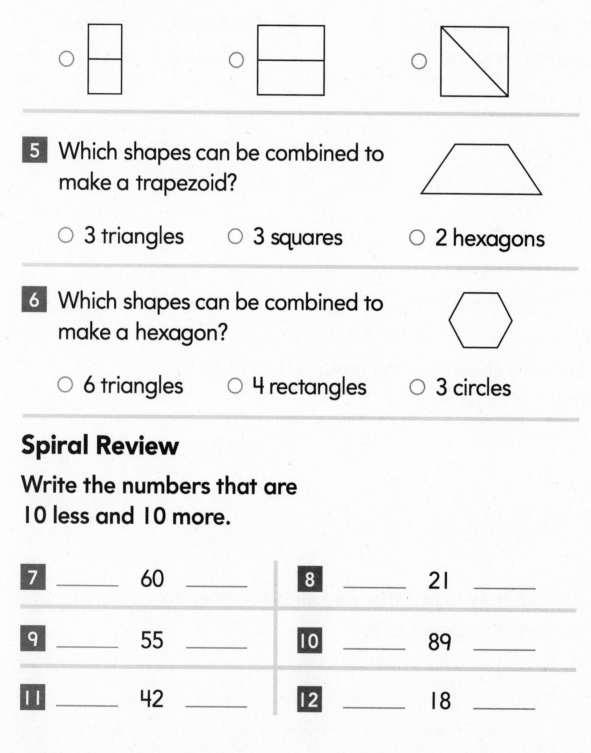

○ ○ ○

5 Which shapes can be combined to make a trapezoid?

○ 3 triangles   ○ 3 squares   ○ 2 hexagons

6 Which shapes can be combined to make a hexagon?

○ 6 triangles   ○ 4 rectangles   ○ 3 circles

Spiral Review

Write the numbers that are 10 less and 10 more.

7 ____ 60 ____   **8** ____ 21 ____

9 ____ 55 ____   **10** ____ 89 ____

11 ____ 42 ____   **12** ____ 18 ____

Name ______________________

LESSON 15.4
More Practice/ Homework

ONLINE
Video Tutorials and Interactive Examples

Identify Composed Shapes

1 **Math on the Spot** Draw lines to show two different ways to combine the shapes on the left to make new shapes on the right.

2 (MP) **Use Structure** Circle the 2 shapes used to make the new shape.

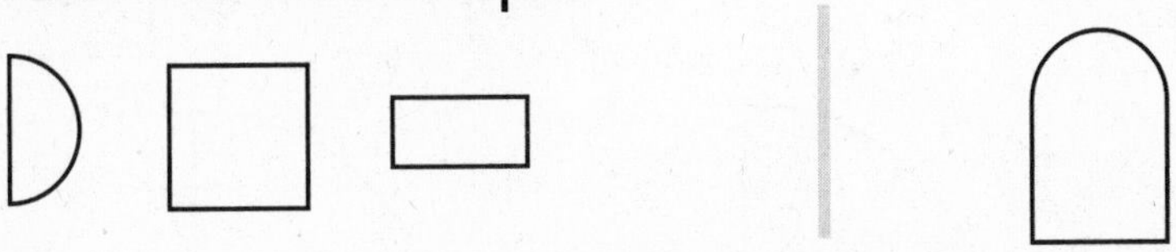

3 **Open Ended** Use these 3 shapes to make a combined shape. Draw your shape.

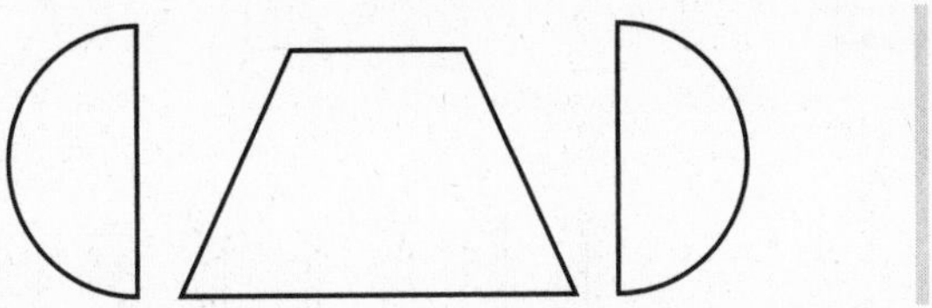

4 (MP) **Attend to Precision** Describe the new shape you make when you combine the two triangles.

____

____

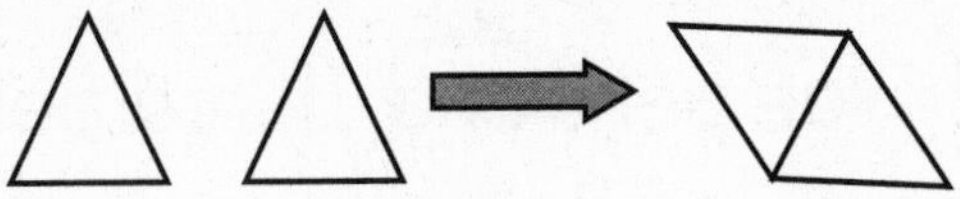

Test Prep

Fill in the bubble next to the correct answer

5 Which shows a trapezoid and a triangle combined to make a large triangle?

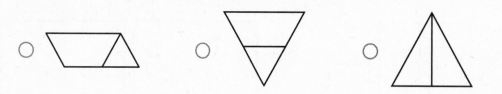

○   ○   ○

6 Harry uses these 2 shapes to make a new shape. Which new shape can he make?

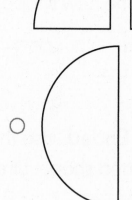

   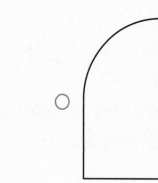

○   ○   ○

Spiral Review

7 Write the number.

_____ tens _____ ones = _____

8 Misha puts 21 blue pens and 14 red pens on the table. How many pens does she put on the table?

_____ pens

LESSON 15.5
**More Practice/
Homework**

ONLINE
Video Tutorials and
Interactive Examples

Make New Two-Dimensional Shapes

1 (MP) **Use Structure**

- Levi combines △ and △ to make ⬦.

- He makes that same shape again.

- He puts his combined shapes together.

Circle the new shape Levi could make.

---

2 (MP) **Use Structure**

- Rae combines ☐ and ▭ to make .

- She makes that same shape again.

- She puts her 2 combined shapes together.

Circle the new shape Rae could make.

Test Prep

Fill in the bubble next to the correct answer.

3 Mark combines a triangle and a trapezoid. Which shape does he make?

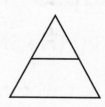

○ hexagon   ○ square   ○ triangle

4 Mark makes the same shape again. He puts his 2 shapes together to make a new larger shape. Which shape could he make?

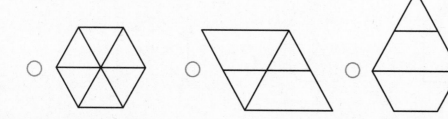

○   ○   ○

Spiral Review

Write the number.

5
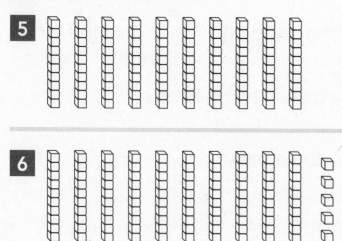

_____

6

_____

Name _____

LESSON 16.1
**More Practice/
Homework**

ONLINE
Video Tutorials and
Interactive Examples

Take Apart Two-Dimensional Shapes

(MP) **Use Structure** Draw lines to show the shapes.

1 Charlie uses 4 shapes that are the same size to make a rectangle.

2 Frank uses 2 shapes that are the same size to make a square.

(MP) **Attend to Precision** Draw triangles, squares, or rectangles to make the shape.

3 Draw 2 shapes the same size and shape to make a rectangle.

4 Draw 4 shapes the same size and shape to make a square.

Test Prep

Fill in the bubble next to the correct answer.

5 Nala draws lines in a rectangle to show
4 shapes that are the same size.
Which is her shape?

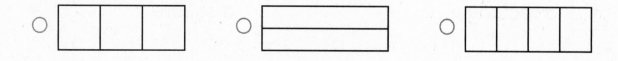

○   ○   ○

6 Simon draws a line in a circle to show
2 shapes that are the same size.
Which is his shape?

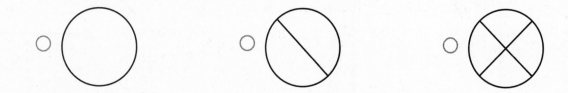

○   ○   ○

Spiral Review

7 Draw to show a hexagon.

How many sides
does a hexagon have?   _____

8 Draw to show a trapezoid.

How many vertices
does a trapezoid have?   _____

© Houghton Mifflin Harcourt Publishing Company

LESSON 16.2
**More Practice/
Homework**

ONLINE
Video Tutorials and
Interactive Examples

Identify Equal or Unequal Shares

1 Draw lines to show
4 equal shares.

2 Draw lines to show
4 unequal shares.

(MP) Construct Arguments
How do you know the
shares are equal?

_____

_____

(MP) Construct Arguments
How do you know the
shares are unequal?

_____

_____

Write equal shares or unequal shares.

3

_____

4

_____

Math on the Spot Write the number of equal shares.

5

_____ equal shares

6

_____ equal shares

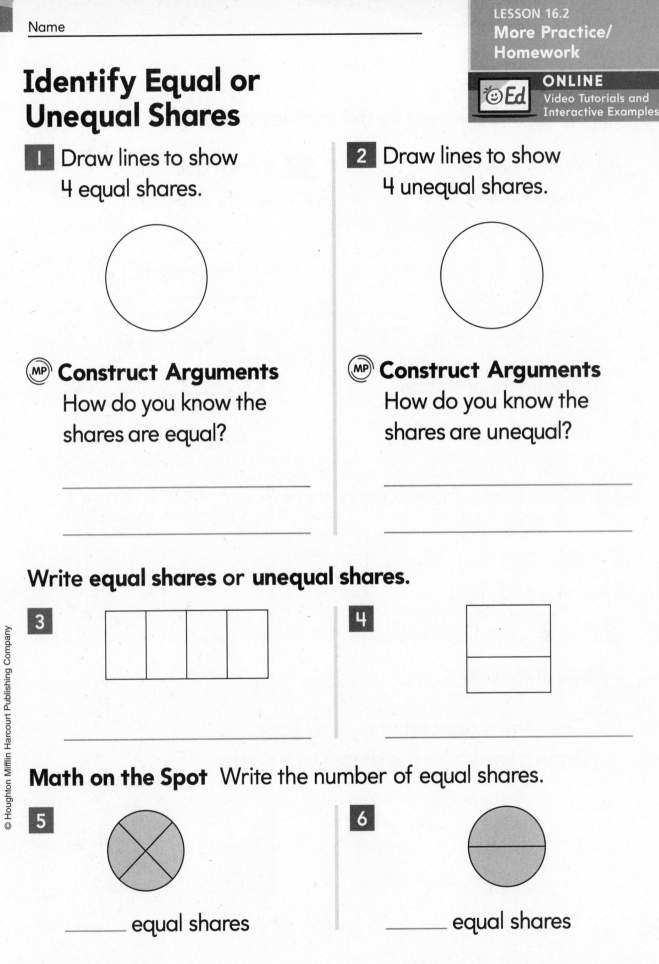

Test Prep

Fill in the bubble next to the correct answer.

7 Which does this shape show?

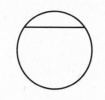

○ 2 equal shares

○ 2 unequal shares

○ 4 unequal shares

8 Which does this shape show?

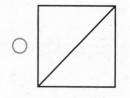

○ 2 equal shares

○ 4 equal shares

○ 4 unequal shares

9 Which shape shows 2 equal shares?

○   ○   ○

Spiral Review

10 Circle the shapes with only 3 vertices.
Draw a line under the shapes with 4 sides.

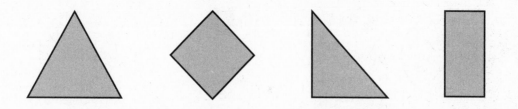

LESSON 16.3
**More Practice/
Homework**

 **ONLINE**
Video Tutorials and
Interactive Examples

Partition Shapes into Halves

(MP) **Use Structure** Draw a line to show halves. Color half of each shape.

1 Rae sees a half moon in the sky. Show two different ways the moon could show halves.

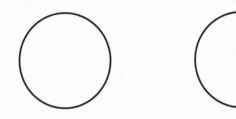

2 Show half of the rectangle.

3 Show half of the square.

4 **Math on the Spot** Use the picture. Write numbers to solve.

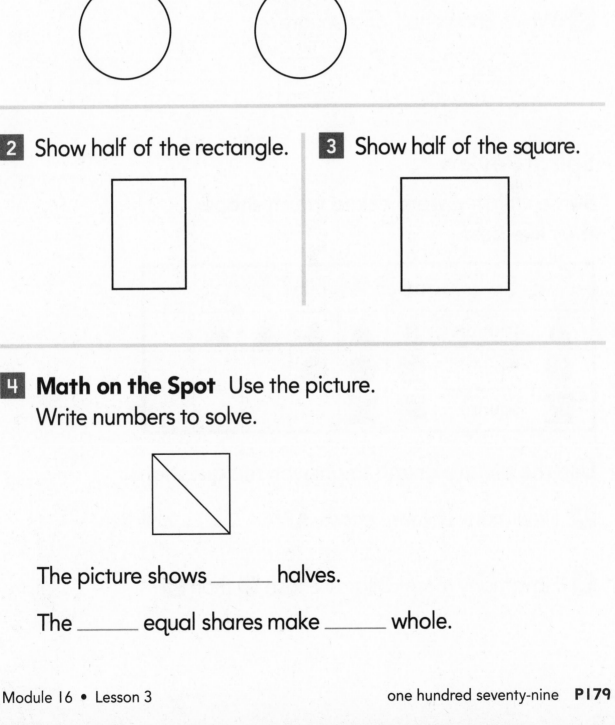

The picture shows _____ halves.

The _____ equal shares make _____ whole.

Test Prep

Fill in the bubble next to the correct answer.

5 Which shape shows halves?

○ ⊘ ○ ⊘ ○ ▭

6 Which shows half of a square?

○ ◇ ○ ▢ ○ ▢

Spiral Review

Some children were asked which shape they like best.

Shapes We Like						
▲ triangle	▲	▲	▲	▲	▲	
● circle	●	●	●			
■ square	■	■				

Use the picture graph to answer the questions.

7 How many children chose ▲? _____ children

8 How many more children chose ● than ■? _____ more

© Houghton Mifflin Harcourt Publishing Company

LESSON 16.4
**More Practice/
Homework**

ONLINE
Video Tutorials and
Interactive Examples

Partition Shapes into Fourths

(MP) **Attend to Precision** Draw lines to show fourths. Color one quarter of the shape.

1

2

3

4 **Math on the Spot** Circle the shape that shows quarters.

Test Prep

Fill in the bubble next to the correct answer.

5 Which shape shows quarters?

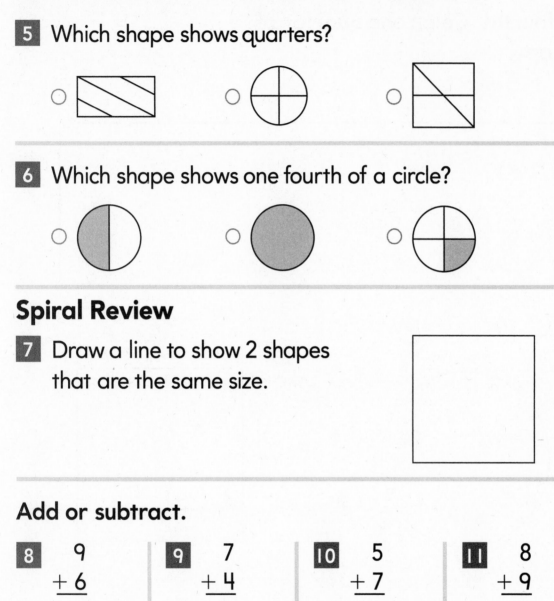

○   ○   ○

6 Which shape shows one fourth of a circle?

○   ○   ○

Spiral Review

7 Draw a line to show 2 shapes that are the same size.

Add or subtract.

8
$$9 + 6$$

9
$$7 + 4$$

10
$$5 + 7$$

11
$$8 + 9$$

12
$$18 - 9$$

13
$$14 - 6$$

14
$$16 - 7$$

15
$$13 - 7$$

LESSON 17.1
**More Practice/
Homework**

🔴Ed **ONLINE**
Video Tutorials and
Interactive Examples

Order Length

1 (MP) **Attend to Precision** Kahn has
3 pencils of different lengths. Draw the
pencils. Circle the longest pencil.

2 Draw 3 lines in order from longest to shortest.

3 Draw 3 lines in order from shortest to longest.

Test Prep

Fill in the bubble next to the correct answer.

4 Sasha draws 3 rectangles. Which is the longest rectangle?

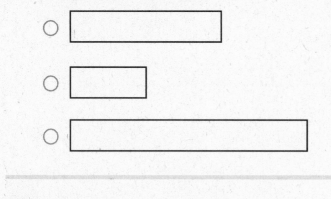

○ ▭

○ ▭

○ ▭

5 Which is the shortest line?

○ ──────

○ ────────

○ ───────

Spiral Review

6 Circle the shape that can be made by combining 3 triangles?

7 Circle the shape that shows equal shares.

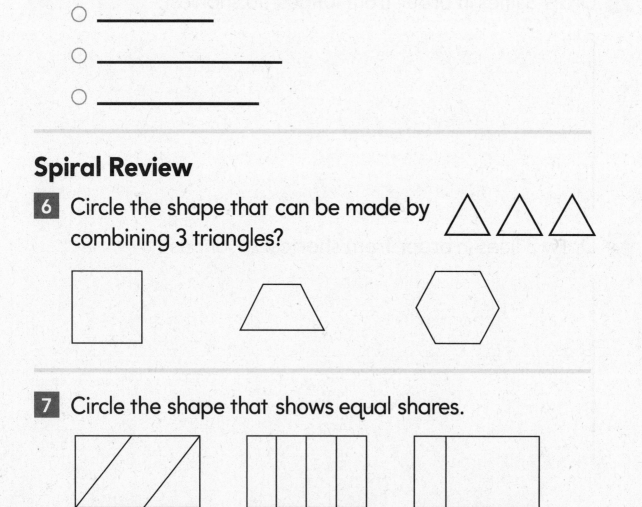

LESSON 17.2
**More Practice/
Homework**

ONLINE
Video Tutorials and
Interactive Examples

Use Indirect Measurement to Compare Length

1 The box is shorter than the gray string.
Draw the length of the box.

The pen is longer than the gray string.
Draw the pen.

Is the pen longer or shorter than the box?

_____

Will the pen fit in the box? _____

2 Read the clues. Write longer or shorter.

A red banner is shorter than a yellow banner.

The yellow banner is shorter than a green banner.

The green banner is _____ than the red banner.

Draw to show your work.

Test Prep

3 There are 3 roses. The red rose is longer than the yellow rose. The purple rose is shorter than the yellow rose. Which sentence is true?

○ The red rose is longer than the purple rose.

○ The red rose is shorter than the purple rose.

○ The red rose is the same length as the purple rose.

Spiral Review

4 Juan makes two of the same combined shape. He combines the shapes to make a larger shape. Draw the shape he could make.

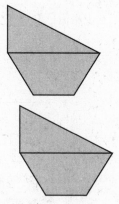

5 Draw lines to show fourths. Color one fourth of the shape.

6 Draw a line to show halves. Color one half of the shape.

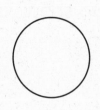

LESSON 17.3
**More Practice/
Homework**

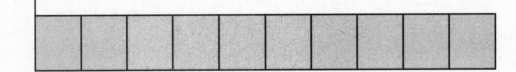

ONLINE
Video Tutorials and
Interactive Examples

Use Nonstandard Units to Measure Length

1 How many units long is the fish?

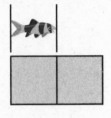

about _____ unit long

---

2 Blake measures a vine to be about 5 tiles long.
Then he measures the vine using shorter units.
Will the measurement using shorter units be
more or less than 5 tiles long. Explain.

_____

_____

---

3 Use the units below. Draw a pencil that is
6 units long.

Test Prep

Fill in the bubble next to the correct answer.

4 How many units long is the nail?

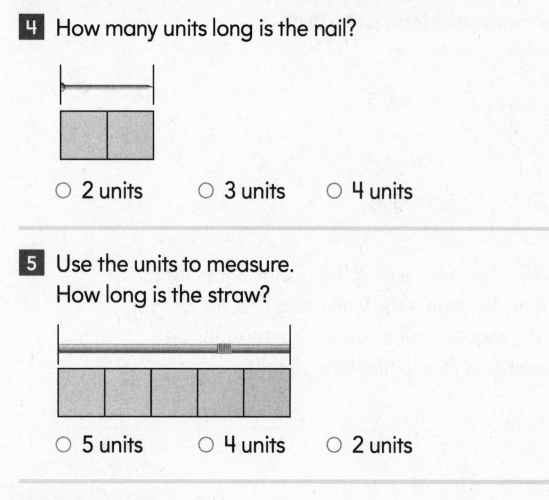

○ 2 units   ○ 3 units   ○ 4 units

---

5 Use the units to measure.
How long is the straw?

○ 5 units   ○ 4 units   ○ 2 units

Spiral Review

6 Circle the shortest pencil.

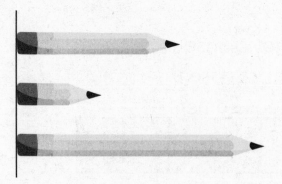

Name _____

LESSON 17.4
More Practice/ Homework

ONLINE
Video Tutorials and
Interactive Examples

Make a Nonstandard Measuring Tool

Use the measuring tool you made to measure the length.

1 How many units long is the toy dinosaur?

about _____ units

---

2 How long is the model train track?

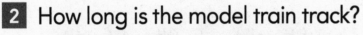

about _____ units

---

3 Compare the length of the toy dinosaur and the length of the train track. Use the > symbol to compare the measurements.

_____ ◯ _____

Test Prep

Fill in the bubble next to the correct answer.
Use the measuring tool to measure the length.

4 How long is the worm?

1	2	3	4

○ about 1 unit   ○ about 2 units   ○ about 3 units

5 How long is the line to the nearest unit?

1	2	3	4	5	6

○ about 4 units   ○ about 5 units   ○ about 6 units

Spiral Review

6 Brice combines 4 of these shapes to make
a new shape. Draw to show the new shape.

Name _____

LESSON 18.1
**More Practice/
Homework**

ONLINE
Video Tutorials and
Interactive Examples

Understand Time to the Hour

1 **Use Structure** Albert eats lunch at
12:00. Which clock shows 12 o'clock?
Circle your answer.

2 **Attend to Precision** Rosa plays
softball at 5:00. Draw the hour hand
to show 5:00.

3 What is the time?

The time is _____ o'clock.

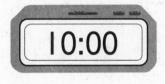

10:00

4 **Math on the Spot** Which time is **not** the
same? Circle it.

3:00   3 o'clock

Test Prep

Fill in the bubble next to the correct answer.

5 Which time does the clock show?

○ 2:00 ○ 6:00 ○ 7:00

6 Which shows 5 o'clock?

○ 4:00 ○ 5:00 ○ 8:00

Spiral Review

7 Chris has 3 ribbons. The purple ribbon is shorter than the yellow ribbon. The blue ribbon is longer than the yellow ribbon.

Draw the ribbons. Write **shorter** or **longer** to complete the sentence.

The blue ribbon is _____ than the purple ribbon.

© Houghton Mifflin Harcourt Publishing Company

Name _____

Understand Time to the Half Hour

1 (MP) **Use Structure** Marlene goes to the movies. She arrives at half past 4:00. Circle the clock that shows the time she arrives.

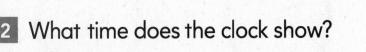

---

2 What time does the clock show?

The time is half past _____.

---

3 **Math on the Spot** Tim plays soccer at half past 8:00. He eats lunch at half past 12:00. He sees a movie at half past 1:00.

Look at the clock.
Write the activity that Tim does at the time shown on the clock.

Tim _____.

Test Prep

Fill in the bubble next to the correct answer.

4 Which time does the clock show?

○ half past 6:00

○ half past 7:00

○ half past 8:00

5 Which clock shows half past 5 o'clock?

 ○    ○    ○

6 Alicia goes to the library at the time shown on the clock. Write the time.

The time is half past _____ o'clock.

Spiral Review

7 How long is the pencil?

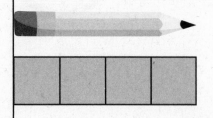

The pencil is about _____ units long.

LESSON 18.3
**More Practice/
Homework**

 ONLINE
Video Tutorials and
Interactive Examples

Tell Time to the Hour and Half Hour

1 Monica wakes up for school at 7:30. Circle the clock that shows the time she wakes up for school.

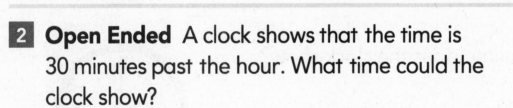

2 **Open Ended** A clock shows that the time is 30 minutes past the hour. What time could the clock show?

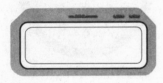

3 **Math on the Spot** Mel goes to the park at half past 2. Which clock shows when Mel goes to the park? Circle the clock that shows the time.

2:00   3:30   2:30

Test Prep

Fill in the bubble next to the correct answer.

4 Which time does the clock show?

○ 6:30   ○ 7:00   ○ 7:30

5 Which time does the clock show?

○ 1:00   ○ 1:30   ○ 6:00

6 Which time does the clock show?

○ 10:00   ○ 12:00   ○ 2:00

Spiral Review

7 What is the time?

8 What is the time?

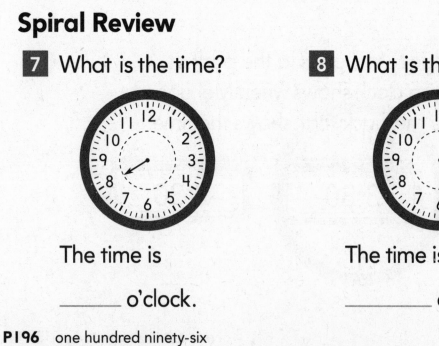

The time is

_____ o'clock.

The time is half past

_____ o'clock.

Practice Time to the Hour and Half Hour

(MP) Use Repeated Reasoning What time does the clock show? Write the time on the digital clock.

1

2

3

4 **Math on the Spot** What is the error? Zoey tried to show 6:00. Explain how to change the clock to show 6:00.

_____

_____

5 Soccer practice begins at 4:30. Draw the hour hand and the minute hand on the clock.

Test Prep

Fill in the bubble next to the correct answer.

6 Which time does the clock show?

○ 11:00
○ 11:30
○ 12:30

---

7 Caroline reads until 8:30. Which clock show 8:30?

○   ○   ○

---

8 The time is 9:30. Which number does the minute hand point to?

○ 6   ○ 9   ○ 12

Spiral Review

Write the time shown on each clock.

9

10

HMH | into Math™

My Journal

My Progress on Mathematics Standards

The lessons in your *Into Math* book provide instruction for Mathematics Standards for Grade 1. You can use the following pages to reflect on your learning and record your progress through the standards.

As you learn new concepts, reflect on this learning. Consider inserting a check mark if you understand the concepts or inserting a question mark if you have questions or need help.

	Student Edition Lessons	My Progress
Domain: OPERATIONS AND ALGEBRAIC THINKING		
Cluster: Represent and solve problems involving addition and subtraction.		
Use addition and subtraction within 20 to solve word problems involving situations of adding to, taking from, putting together, taking apart, and comparing, with unknowns in all positions, e.g., by using objects, drawings, and equations with a symbol for the unknown number to represent the problem.	1.1, 1.7, 2.1, 2.6, 4.6, 5.1, 5.2, 5.3, 5.4, 6.1, 6.2, 6.3, 6.4, 6.5, 6.6, 6.7, 7.1, 7.2, 7.3, 7.4, 7.5, 7.6, 7.7	
Solve word problems that call for addition of three whole numbers whose sum is less than or equal to 20, e.g., by using objects, drawings, and equations with a symbol for the unknown number to represent the problem.	3.3, 3.4, 3.5	

	Student Edition Lessons	My Progress
Cluster: Understand and apply properties of operations and the relationship between addition and subtraction.		
Apply properties of operations as strategies to add and subtract.	3.1, 3.2, 3.3, 3.4, 3.5	
Understand subtraction as an unknown-addend problem.	2.4, 4.1	
Cluster: Add and subtract within 20.		
Relate counting to addition and subtraction (e.g., by counting on 2 to add 2).	1.2, 2.2, 2.3	
Add and subtract within 20, demonstrating fluency for addition and subtraction within 10. Use strategies such as counting on; making ten (e.g., $8 + 6 = 8 + 2 + 4 = 10 + 4 = 14$); decomposing a number leading to a ten (e.g., $13 - 4 = 13 - 3 - 1 = 10 - 1 = 9$); using the relationship between addition and subtraction (e.g., knowing that $8 + 4 = 12$, one knows $12 - 8 = 4$); and creating equivalent but easier or known sums (e.g., adding $6 + 7$ by creating the known equivalent $6 + 6 + 1 = 12 + 1 = 13$).	1.3, 1.4, 1.5, 1.6, 1.7, 2.4, 2.5, 2.6, 3.7, 4.1, 4.2, 4.3, 4.4, 4.7, 13.5	
Cluster: Work with addition and subtraction equations.		
Understand the meaning of the equal sign, and determine if equations involving addition and subtraction are true or false.	3.6, 11.3	
Determine the unknown whole number in an addition or subtraction equation relating to three whole numbers.	2.4, 4.1, 4.5, 4.6	

	Student Edition Lessons	My Progress
Domain: NUMBER AND OPERATIONS IN BASE TEN		
Cluster: Extend the counting sequence.		
Count to 120, starting at any number less than 120. In this range, read and write numerals and represent a number of objects with a written numeral.	10.1, 10.5, 10.6	
Cluster: Understand place value.		
Understand that the two digits of a two-digit number represent amounts of tens and ones.	10.2, 10.3	
• 10 can be thought of as a bundle of ten ones — called a "ten."	9.1, 9.2, 9.3, 10.4	
• The numbers from 11 to 19 are composed of a ten and one, two, three, four, five, six, seven, eight, or nine ones.	9.1, 9.2	
• The numbers 10, 20, 30, 40, 50, 60, 70, 80, 90 refer to one, two, three, four, five, six, seven, eight, or nine tens (and 0 ones).	9.3	
Compare two two-digit numbers based on meanings of the tens and ones digits, recording the results of comparisons with the symbols >, =, and <.	11.1, 11.2, 11.3, 11.4	

	Student Edition Lessons	My Progress
Cluster: Use place value understanding and properties of operations to add and subtract.		
Add within 100, including adding a two-digit number and a one-digit number, and adding a two-digit number and a multiple of 10, using concrete models or drawings and strategies based on place value, properties of operations, and/or the relationship between addition and subtraction; relate the strategy to a written method and explain the reasoning used. Understand that in adding two-digit numbers, one adds tens and tens, ones and ones; and sometimes it is necessary to compose a ten.	12.1, 12.3, 12.4, 12.5, 12.6, 12.7, 13.1, 13.2, 13.4, 13.6	
Given a two-digit number, mentally find 10 more or 10 less than the number, without having to count; explain the reasoning used.	12.8	
Subtract multiples of 10 in the range 10-90 from multiples of 10 in the range 10-90 (positive or zero differences), using concrete models or drawings and strategies based on place value, properties of operations, and/or the relationship between addition and subtraction; relate the strategy to a written method and explain the reasoning used.	12.2, 12.3, 13.1, 13.3, 13.4, 13.6	

	Student Edition Lessons	My Progress
Domain: MEASUREMENT AND DATA		
Cluster: Measure lengths indirectly and by iterating length units.		
Order three objects by length; compare the lengths of two objects indirectly by using a third object.	17.1, 17.2	
Express the length of an object as a whole number of length units, by laying multiple copies of a shorter object (the length unit) end to end; understand that the length measurement of an object is the number of same-size length units that span it with no gaps or overlaps.	17.3, 17.4	
Cluster: Tell and write time.		
Tell and write time in hours and half-hours using analog and digital clocks.	18.1, 18.2, 18.3, 18.4	
Cluster: Represent and interpret data.		
Organize, represent, and interpret data with up to three categories; ask and answer questions about the total number of data points, how many in each category, and how many more or less are in one category than in another.	8.1, 8.2, 8.3, 8.4, 8.5, 8.6, 8.7	

	Student Edition Lessons	My Progress
Domain: GEOMETRY		
Cluster: Reason with shapes and their attributes.		
Distinguish between defining attributes (e.g., triangles are closed and three-sided) versus non-defining attributes (e.g., color, orientation, overall size); build and draw shapes to possess defining attributes.	14.1, 15.1, 15.2	
Compose two-dimensional shapes (rectangles, squares, trapezoids, triangles, half-circles, and quarter-circles) or three-dimensional shapes (cubes, right rectangular prisms, right circular cones, and right circular cylinders) to create a composite shape, and compose new shapes from the composite shape.	14.2, 14.3, 15.3, 15.4, 15.5	
Partition circles and rectangles into two and four equal shares, describe the shares using the words *halves*, *fourths*, and *quarters*, and use the phrases *half of*, *fourth of*, and *quarter of*. Describe the whole as two of, or four of the shares. Understand for these examples that decomposing into more equal shares creates smaller shares.	16.1, 16.2, 16.3, 16.4	

My Learning Summary

As you learn about new concepts, complete a learning summary for each module. A learning summary can include drawings, examples, non-examples, and terminology. It's your learning summary, so show or include information that will help you.

At the end of each module, you will have a summary you can reference to review content for a module test and help you make connections with related math concepts.

My Learning Summary

My Learning Summary

My Learning Summary

My Learning Summary

My Learning Summary

My Learning Summary

My Learning Summary

My Learning Summary

My Learning Summary

My Learning Summary

My Learning Summary

My Learning Summary

My Learning Summary

My Learning Summary

My Learning Summary

My Learning Summary

Name _____

My Learning Summary

My Learning Summary

As you learn about each new term, add notes, drawings, or sentences in the space next to the definition. Doing so will help you remember what each term means.

A	**My Vocabulary Summary**
add **sumar** **Add** to find how many altogether. 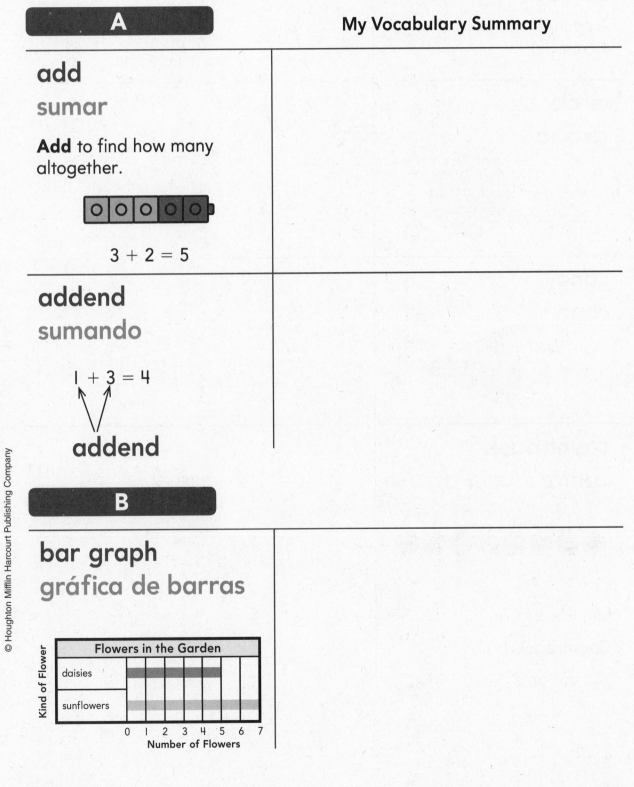 3 + 2 = 5	
addend **sumando** I + 3 = 4 **addend**	

B

bar graph
gráfica de barras

Flowers in the Garden							
daisies							
sunflowers							

Kind of Flower

0 1 2 3 4 5 6 7

Number of Flowers

Interactive Glossary

My Vocabulary Summary

cent (¢)
centavo

A penny has a value of
1 **cent** (1¢).

circle
círculo

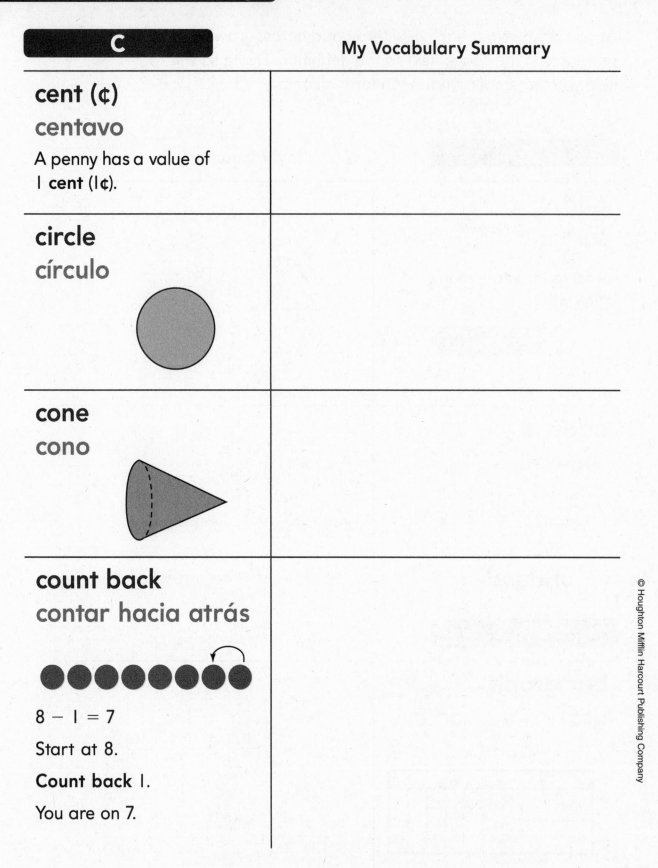

cone
cono

count back
contar hacia atrás

8 − 1 = 7

Start at 8.

Count back 1.

You are on 7.

My Vocabulary Summary

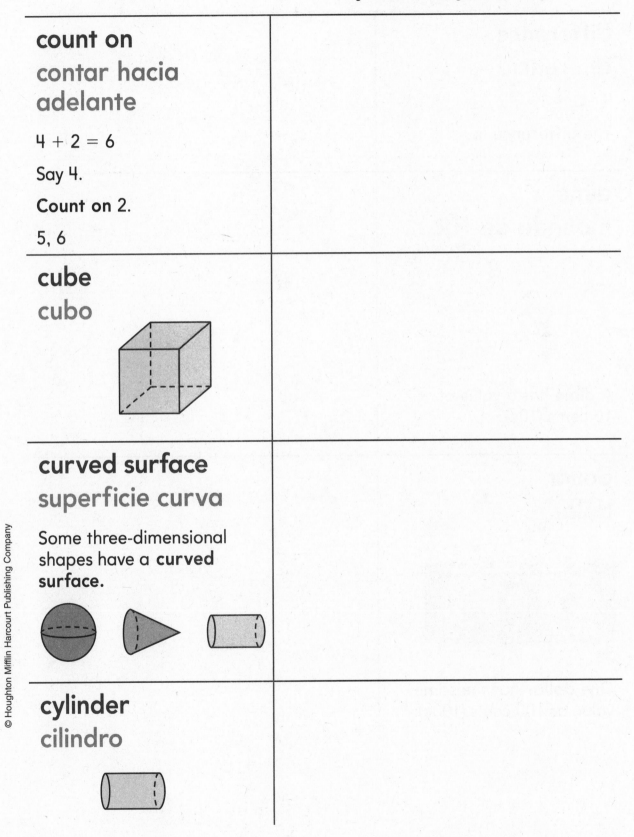

count on

contar hacia adelante

$4 + 2 = 6$

Say 4.

Count on 2.

5, 6

cube

cubo

curved surface

superficie curva

Some three-dimensional shapes have a **curved surface.**

cylinder

cilindro

D	My Vocabulary Summary
difference diferencia 4 − 3 = 1 The **difference** is 1.	
dime moneda de 10¢ A **dime** has a value of 10 cents (10¢).	
dollar dólar One **dollar** has the same value as 100 cents (100¢).	

My Vocabulary Summary

doubles
dobles

$5 + 5 = 10$

E

equal shares
partes iguales

These show equal parts, or **equal shares**.

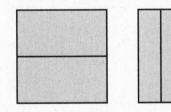

equation
ecuación

$7 = 5 + 2$ is an example of an addition **equation**.

$8 - 5 = 3$ is an example of a subtraction **equation**.

F

fewer
menos

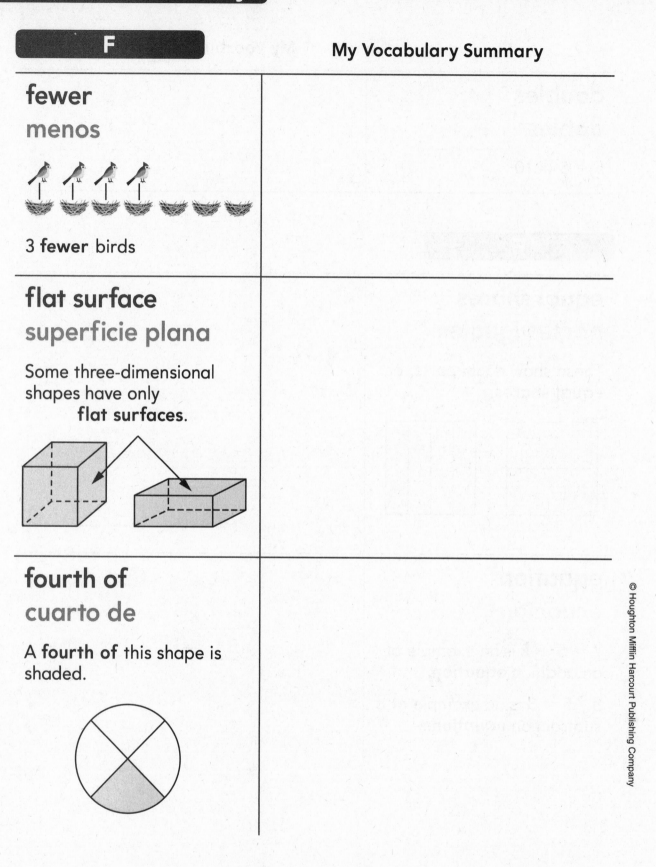

3 **fewer** birds

flat surface
superficie plana

Some three-dimensional shapes have only **flat surfaces.**

fourth of
cuarto de

A **fourth of** this shape is shaded.

My Vocabulary Summary

fourths
cuartos

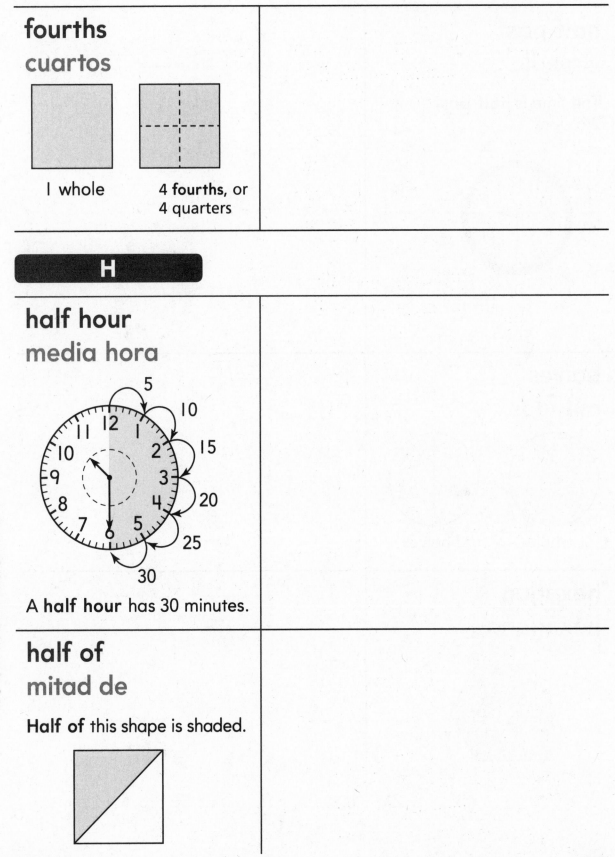

| I whole | 4 **fourths**, or 4 quarters |

H

half hour
media hora

A **half hour** has 30 minutes.

half of
mitad de

Half of this shape is shaded.

My Vocabulary Summary

half past
y media

The time is **half past** 2 o'clock.

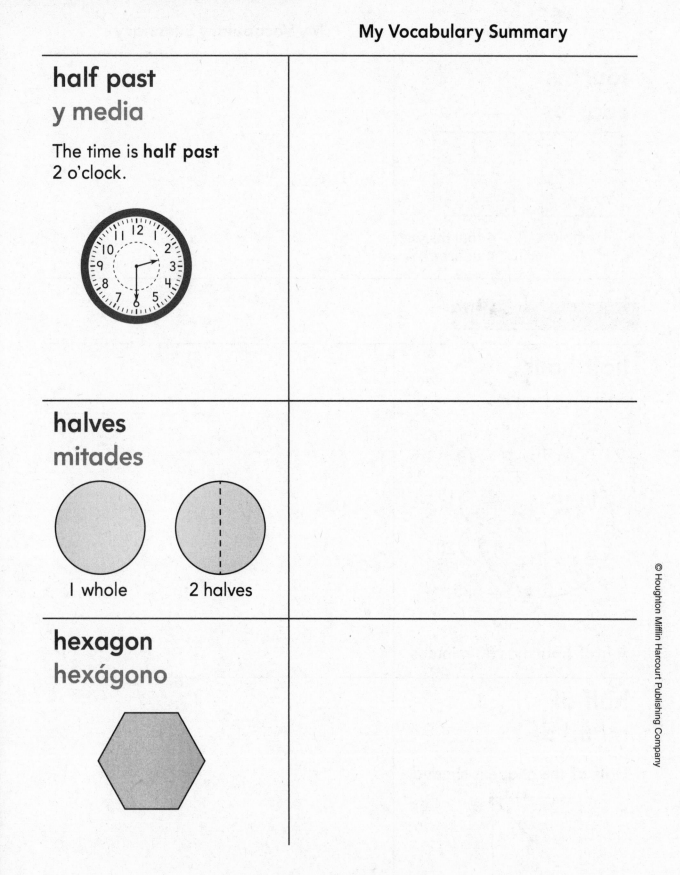

halves
mitades

I whole   2 halves

hexagon
hexágono

My Vocabulary Summary

hour
hora

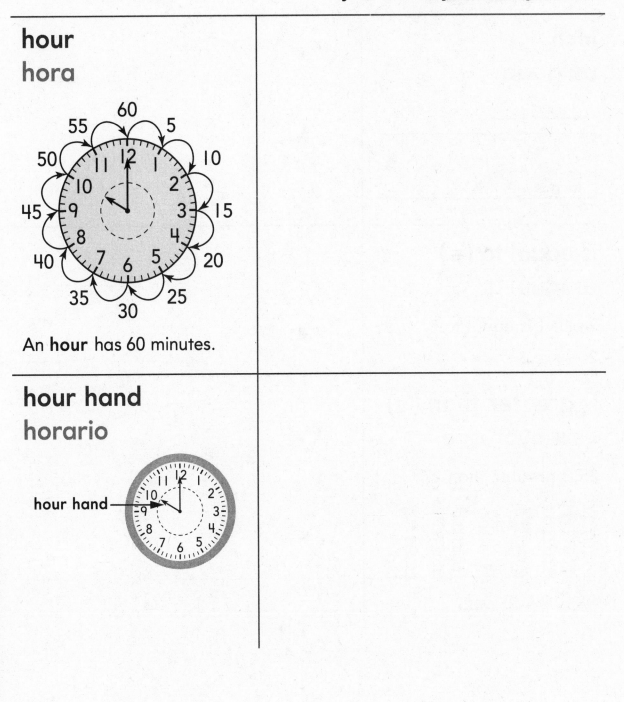

An **hour** has 60 minutes.

hour hand
horario

hour hand →

I

My Vocabulary Summary

inch
pulgada

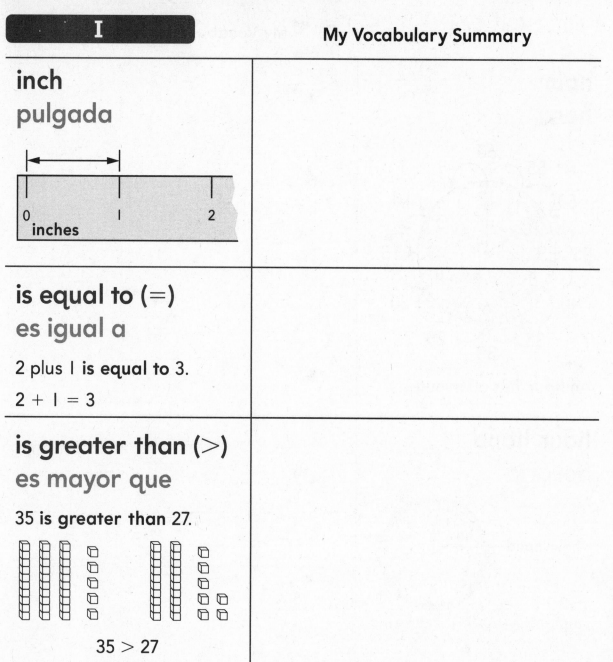

is equal to (=)
es igual a

2 plus 1 **is equal to** 3.

2 + 1 = 3

is greater than (>)
es mayor que

35 **is greater than** 27.

35 > 27

© Houghton Mifflin Harcourt Publishing Company

My Vocabulary Summary

is less than (<)
es menor que

43 is less than 49.

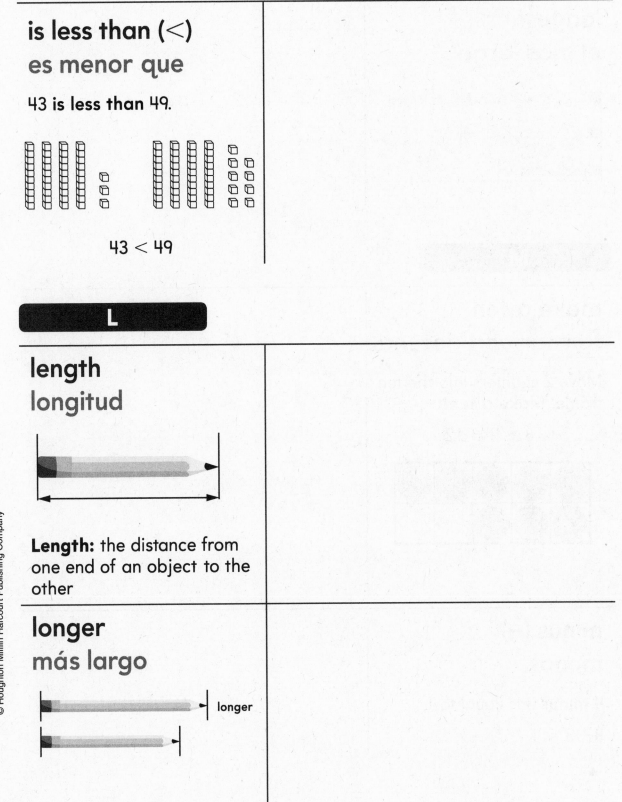

43 < 49

L

length
longitud

Length: the distance from one end of an object to the other

longer
más largo

longer

My Vocabulary Summary

longest
el más largo

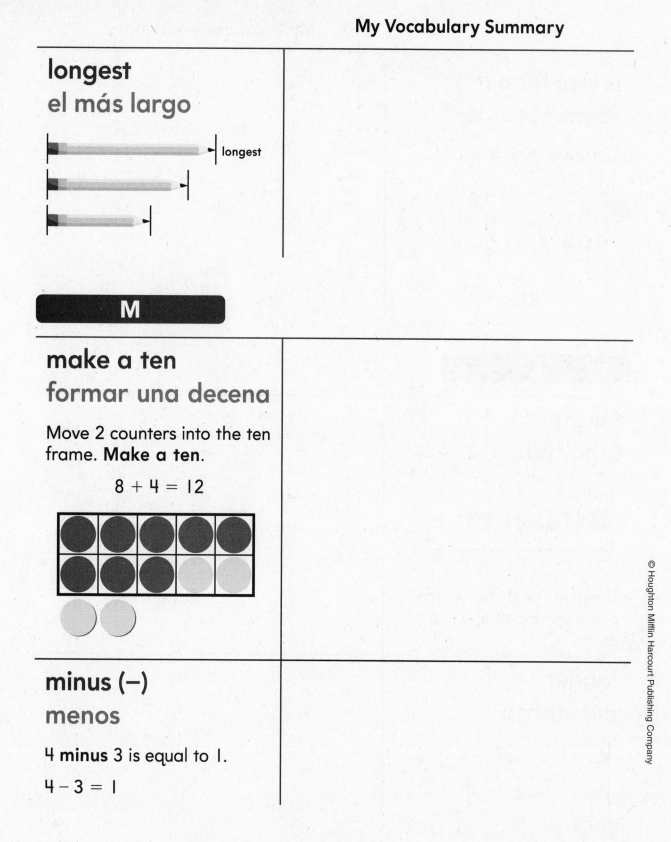

longest

M

make a ten
formar una decena

Move 2 counters into the ten frame. **Make a ten.**

$$8 + 4 = 12$$

---

minus (−)
menos

4 **minus** 3 is equal to 1.

$$4 - 3 = 1$$

My Vocabulary Summary

minute hand
minutero

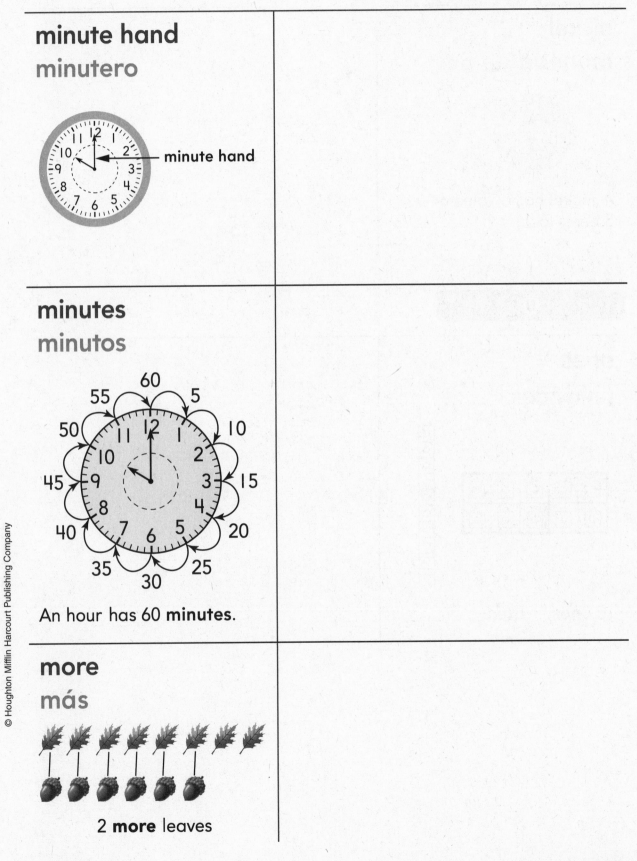

— minute hand

minutes
minutos

An hour has 60 **minutes**.

more
más

2 **more** leaves

N

My Vocabulary Summary

nickel
moneda de 5¢

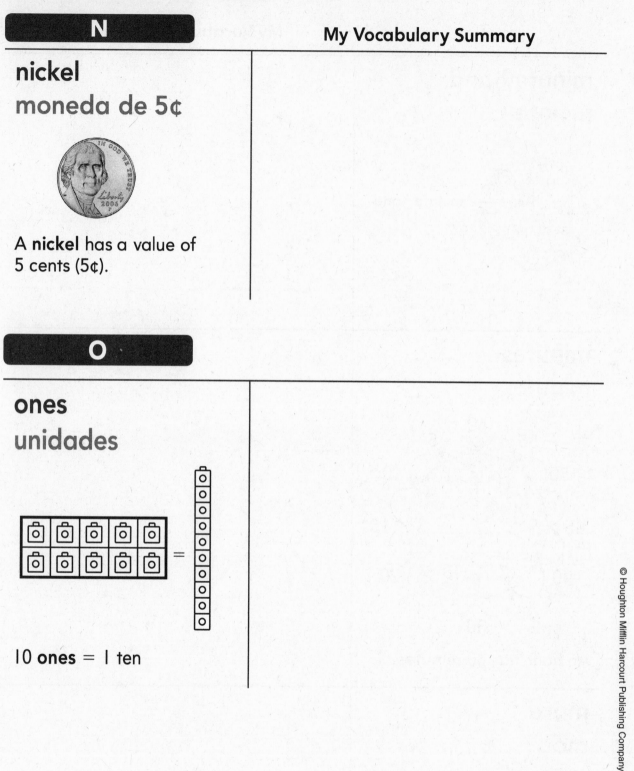

A **nickel** has a value of
5 cents (5¢).

O

ones
unidades

10 **ones** = 1 ten

P

penny
moneda de 1¢

A **penny** has a value of
1 cent (1¢).

picture graph
pictografía

Flowers in the Garden						
✳ daisy	✳	✳	✳			
🌷 tulip	🌷	🌷	🌷	🌷	🌷	

plus (+)
más

2 **plus** 1 is equal to 3.
2 + 1 = 3

Q

quarter

moneda de 25¢

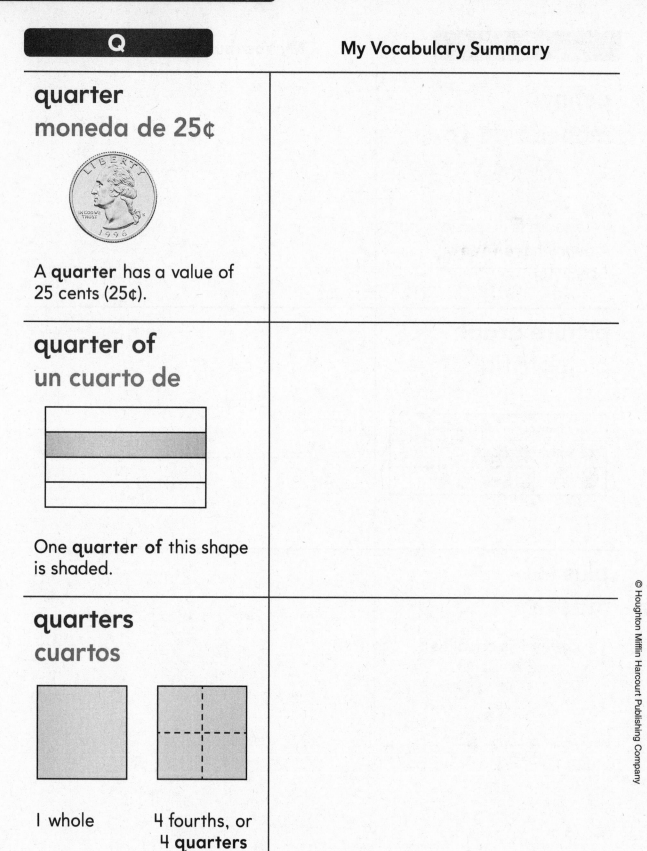

A **quarter** has a value of 25 cents (25¢).

quarter of

un cuarto de

One **quarter of** this shape is shaded.

quarters

cuartos

I whole

4 fourths, or 4 **quarters**

R

rectangle
rectángulo

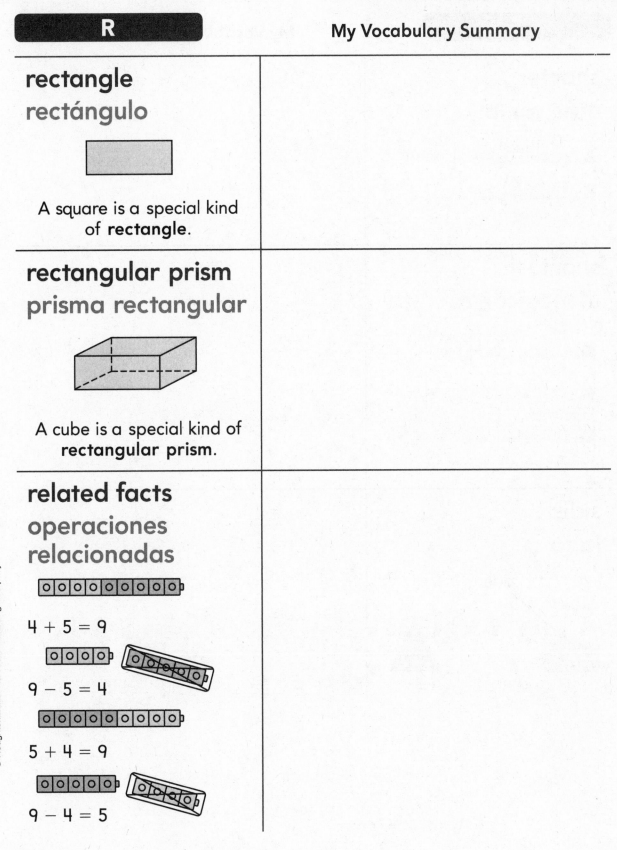

A square is a special kind of **rectangle**.

rectangular prism
prisma rectangular

A cube is a special kind of **rectangular prism**.

related facts
operaciones relacionadas

$4 + 5 = 9$

$9 - 5 = 4$

$5 + 4 = 9$

$9 - 4 = 5$

S

shorter

más corto

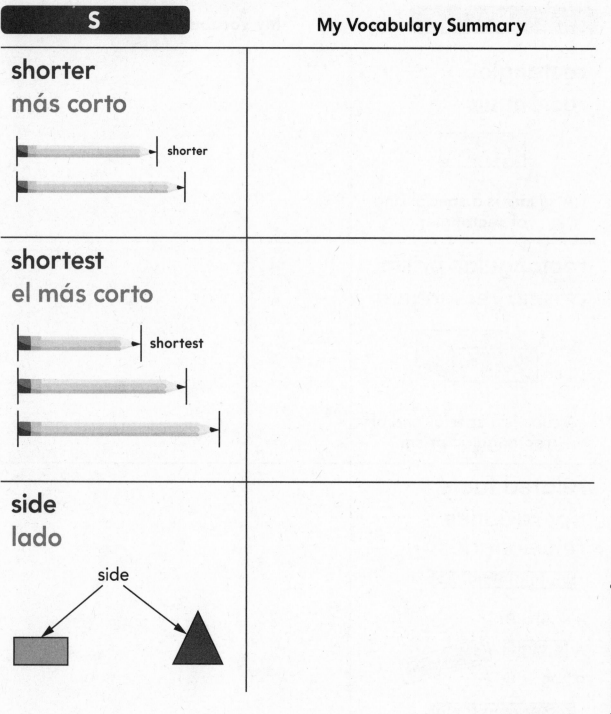

shortest

el más corto

side

lado

My Vocabulary Summary

sphere

esfera

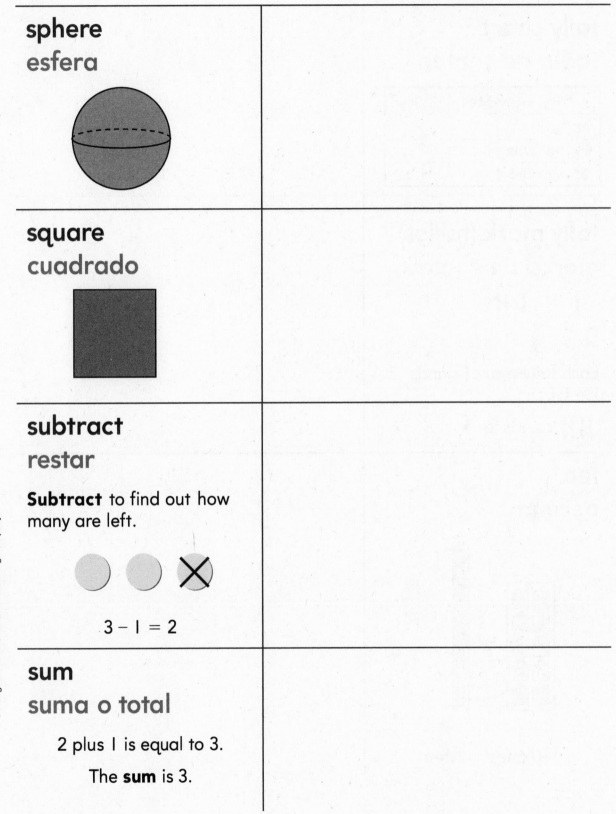

square

cuadrado

subtract

restar

Subtract to find out how many are left.

$3 - 1 = 2$

sum

suma o total

2 plus 1 is equal to 3.

The **sum** is 3.

T

tally chart
tabla de conteo

Toys on the Shelf		Total
bus	I	
car	ⵌ III	
truck	ⵌ I	

tally mark (tallies)
marca de conteo

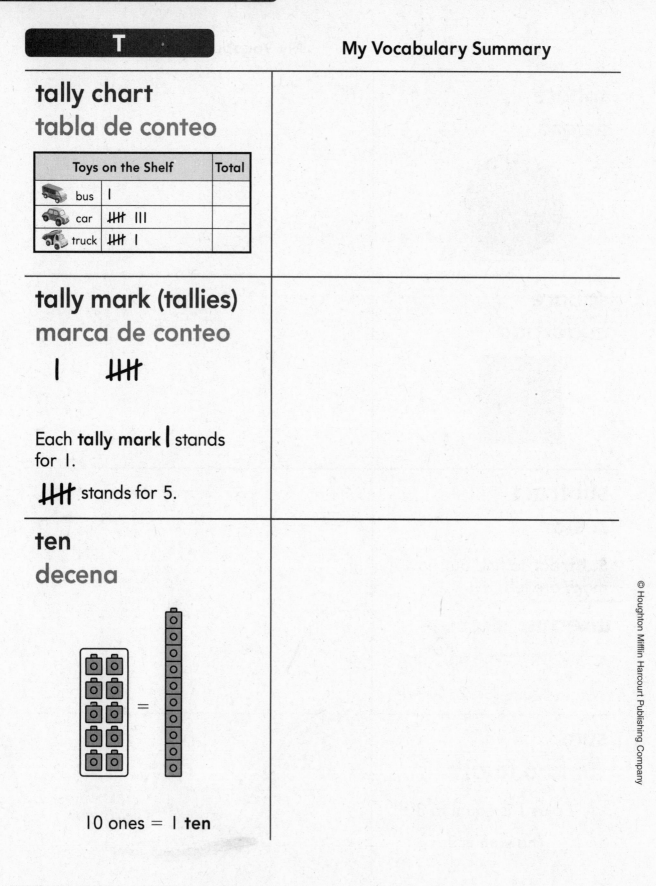

Each **tally mark** I stands for I.

ⵌ stands for 5.

ten
decena

10 ones = I **ten**

My Vocabulary Summary

trapezoid
trapecio

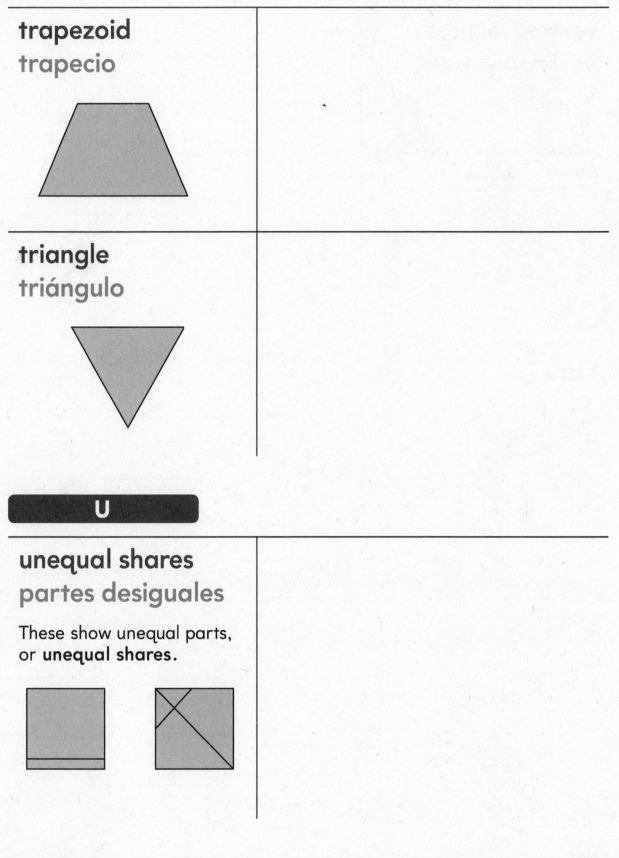

triangle
triángulo

U

unequal shares
partes desiguales

These show unequal parts, or **unequal shares.**

vertex/vertices
vértice/vértices

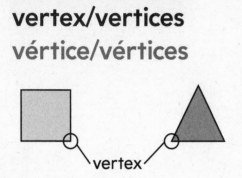

vertex

My Vocabulary Summary